A Salty HAT AND I

CONTENTS:

CHAPTER 1.   CHILDHOOD MEMORIES.

CHAPTER 2.   I MUST GO INTO THE WATER TODAY .

CHAPTER 3.   BUY WISELY, BE SELECTIVE AND Do YOUR RESEARCH.

CHAPTER 4.   WIND , WAVES AND WEATHER.

CHAPTER 5.   THERE'S ALWAYS ANOTHER DAY.

CHAPTER 6.   EVERYONE NEEDS A HERO.

CHAPTER 7.   HEALTH AND WELL BEING.

CHAPTER 8.   A SWIMMER'S BLOG.

CHAPTER 9.   MAKING A DISTANCE SWIM.

CHAPTER 10.   THE IMPORTANCE OF A GOAL.

EPILOGUE.   LOOKING TO THE FUTURE.

NB. this book is deliberately not page numbered. LET'S forget time for a while.

Stephen Hawking.1942—2018.

Portrait by Gillon Lockett.

To Stephen and his family. Thank you Stephen for the hope and inspiration when I needed it most.You've left behind an inspiring legacy.

A beautiful evening on Mylor creek.

A SALTY HAT AND I.

Preface: I have always looked for further information when pursuing a new interest. My favourite reference choice will forever be a good book. However although there are many books on Wild and Distance swimming I failed to find a back to basics one. This information can save a lot of time, unfortunate experiences (I do wish someone had mentioned to me about seasickness in swimmers YUK!) and expense.

I wanted to find little tips which would be invaluable to my swim.

So here is my ABC of the Swimming experience complete with little tips which I often learnt the hard way and suffered as a result. But when all's

said and done one person's swim is individual to them. So I recommend you learn what you want and feel to learn from my book and then get out there and experience what works for you.

2 photos of Castle Point being it's usual angry self.

Go experience the thrill, delight, challenge and satisfaction of Wild water swimming.

HAPPY DAYS X

CHAPTER 1:Childhood memories.

Mummy and I on Castle beach.I was 6 months old.

As a child I lived just a stone's throw from Swanpool beach in Falmouth, Cornwall. A beautiful, safe cove which is a joy to behold. Mummy would take us to the beach at 6am when we had the entire place to ourselves, it felt like home. We would explore every inch of it and spent endless happy times investigating what 'LAY BENEATH' the sea, stones and weed.

My beloved Swanpool Beach on a rough sea day.

I taught myself to swim at around 6 years of age.

Firstly, I would walk on my hands, kicking my feet up and down. Gradually I would lift one hand which produced a somewhat lopsided movement. But oh the thrill of feeling the water supporting me and the realisation that I was moving forward, and not sinking to the seabed.

Note the old tin bucket.

I can't remember exactly when I first lifted both hands at once and reproduced a frantic doggie paddle but I was very soon moving under my own steam. OH, the joy ,oh the excitement I ran up the beach and insisted that Mother and all the family came to see and watch me in action.

The swanpool Swans

The only limitation seemed to be how long I could hold my nerve and the belief that I could indeed move through the water. It was always reassuring to feel the sand again as I stood up, it made me know that all was well and I was in control.

On reflection, I see that at this time my instant and lifetime love of swimming was born.

Ps. All the local kids loved to swim, because the sea was so clean in those days it counted as our bath for the day. YES !!

Swanpool lake

The picture above is Swanpool Lake which is the only water way in Falmouth which nobody swims. It's a Nature reserve and was separated from Swanpool beach by a natural sand bar in

In the Iron Age.

The present road is built on the sand bar.

We had a really rough weather weekend with gale force winds. If you were in or on the water this big wave would be hard and dangerous to deal with.

I love Cornwall in the storms. We wrap up and walk across the beaches. When we were young my brothers would go searching for 'presents from the sea.' This could be anything from wood to the old glass buoys that the fisher men used. The boys built a small boat of wood they gathered from the sea.

The swans have their signets on the Nature reserve but at other times of the year are frequently found on the Beach swimming with the people. Everyone loves them.

CHAPTER 2: I MUST GO INTO THE WATER TODAY.

The sea has always drawn me. All my life the sea and beaches have provided FREE endless, thrilling entertainment.

Deep water is a particular love to me and the solitude of a few in the great deep is both fascinating and thrilling all at the same time. It's a chance to connect with this beautiful World of ours and observe it from a different aspect to the competitive urban life of our People's normality. Out here I see life lived in a wild but natural way.

An example of this was when I saw an altercation between a seagull and a heron while both were on the wing. They seemed furious with each other. Jiving and diving as the seagull dragged the heron by the wing, down, down and down. But the Heron has strong and powerful legs which he put to good use to land a mighty kick to the Gull's chest. This caused a flurry of feathers and an instant break in combat between the opponents and both birds momentarily paused to assess the situation.

But not enough had been done to rent the anger and simultaneously they banged heads and chests and pushed against each other in a bid to gain the upper hand. Amazingly this was all done in utter silence. Only the noise of impact was heard. No shrieking or squawking just intent combat to get the advantage.

As quickly as it started it was over. Both opponents seemingly to agree to disagree. Neither bird had sustained real injury, they parted company and got on with their day.

I will always wonder what the disagreement was about?

They were evenly matched and neither dominated the other. This all happened at around 4.30 am on a Summers day. The tide was full and the sun just rising.I felt privileged to be there.

It's always been a somewhat spooky wonder to me how a sea creature can move with such stealth without me having the slightest inkling they are there. You don't see, hear or feel them coming towards you and it's a startling surprise when they pop up next to you. It's a joy and a major brag that you want to tell everyone but I think a swimmer would be lying if they didn't admit to being cautious and alert.

In the Mylor creek, there is a very large solitary male seal who the locals have christened Sammy. One day Sammy surfaced against my shoulder and let out a massive 'Blow.' Phew, nothing wrong with my heart! But a huge surprise never the less, I hadn't heard or sensed his presence but just all of a sudden he was there eek!! Instantly I said a fervent prayer that he would move away from me. This he did and from a five foot space he mimicked my swim. If I swam Sammy swam, if I stopped he stopped. At one point we observed each other from the distance and momentarily locked eyes. In his eyes I saw a benevolence of a wise old owl and curiosity but no aggression. Just as well as Sammy is huge ,I wouldn't have stood a chance if he had attacked. I talked to him, telling him what a handsome gentleman he is and how I wish I could swim as well as he can. He was listening intently and seemed almost amused and then quite unexpectantly he was gone as covertly as he arrived. Wow ,what an experience one that happens quite often now when he joins me in my swim. I am thrilled but always maintain an air of caution, especially since a friend wickedly recounted a true story of a seal who tried to mate a female swimmer. Holy molie apparently a good punch on the snowt is the order of the day. (Thanks for sharing that with me Nick.) I always wear my buoy so it sits on my back just to make such an event more difficult.

During the course of writing this book I have endeavoured to get a photo of Sammy but to no avail....I keep trying.

Mylor creek has the most lovely echo in the surrounding shoreline. If I shout to ask someone the time or such my voice echoes around and around the area .It's delightful and charming all at the same time.

From my swimming I can say that encounters with wildlife are a regular experience of the distance swimmer. Of course in England this is fairly safe but always with a twist of caution.

Mylor Creek at low tide

The appearance of Sammy on my son Gareth's swim decided Gareth to leave the water asap.

To this day he maintains Sammy is a killer! It's become a family joke.

With climate change we are seeing more and more exotic creatures in our local seas such as the massive but completely harmless basking shark, pods of dolphins are regular visitors though I've never heard of them joining swimmers. The occasional whale makes an appearance and there have been sightings of dustbin jellyfish so called because of their shape, tuna fish and Portuguese man of war. Definitely one to avoid because of their deadly stinging tentacles .If something unusual or best-avoided visits the area the local news will cover the story and sea users are excellent at warning fellow users of the type and location of the creatures. I love the Wild swimming community. Everyone shares a passion and enthusiasm for the water. They might be old, young or in between but they are all lovely and friendly. Always happy to chat and share their experiences. They are the happiest, most helpful group of people ever.

One thing that really inspires and awes me about all sea life is their ability in the sea. I've tried to keep up with fish when snorkelling but once spooked there's no way <u>any</u> swimmer can keep pace. Their magnificent agility is amazing and it's clear they are perfectly engineered for their environment.

I was raised by the sea, we spent long hours enjoying Swanpool beach. We grew to love the sea with all her faces and were taught very early on to always respect her .I will chose the sea above any other water to swim in. To me the sea is alive and independent, it's the biggest natural phenomenon on Mother Earth and yet the least explored. I confess the sea can spook me but I enjoy this edgy relationship I share with her.

SHE SCARES ME ,SHE DARES ME.

Every encounter is different and over time a catalogue of experiences log in a swimmer's mind to be called on to enjoy .This lifetime log is priceless and mustn't be undervalued.

I think of my hero Martin Strel. Everyone marvels that he didn't start his marathon swimming till later in life. But they mustn't forget Martin's life time association with the sea. He states the sea became part of his life at an early age and a good friend for his safety as a refuge from his Father's anger.

When starting out distance swimming I already had massive experience of the sea which perhaps the experts and coaches didn't understand the value of as much as they should have. It might be that you have messed around and swum for pleasure all your life. I can tell you all this experience will really help you as you embark on this new phase of the swim.

If you are totally new or perhaps even scared of the sea I salute you for trying something new. I would strongly recommend you join a cold water club where you will find lots of help and friendship.

Think of the sea as a living entity ,its alive and you have to learn about her and respect her

ways. Get to know her and slowly fall in love. But always treat her with respect.

Mylor creek.

Carrick roads or the big shipping lanes. They run as deep as 34m in the south.

Falmouth Bay on the Castle side.

CHAPTER 3: Buy wisely, be selective and do your research. When buying gear I would definitely

recommend that you look around, ask around and shop around.

It's whatever you feel comfortable in I so admire those who just wear a swimming costume(if you swim the Channel you are only allowed to wear a swimming costume or trunks) but I'm most comfortable in black, skin tight sports gear or a triathlon suit. I HATE wetsuits.I think they are the most uncomfortable things in the world but each to their own. If you are planning on buying a wetsuit really do your homework. You could even perhaps hire one for a while and see how you get along. There are different suits for different sports and different thicknesses of suits for all seasons it's important to get the right one. Of course a wet suit will keep you warm and helps with bouncy keeping the legs up near the surface of the sea. This all adds up to a stronger and more stylish swim. You can also have them measured to you but this is expensive.

 DO YOUR RESEARCH.

There is a terrific second hand market in wet suits which is great. So many people give up before they get started and sell their nearly new gear for a fraction of the cost. But do try it on before you buy.

SEA BOOTS :

When I first started distance swimming I would go bare foot but I quickly found that sea boots are a must. I seriously cut the instep of my foot early on which took forever to heal and was very painful OUCH! Also, the extremities i.e. hands and feet get very cold.

I bought a smashing pair of sea boots with side zips. Zips are a big advantage when taking the boots off with cold hands. BUT I quickly realised that in paying £25 for them I paid too much, there are very similar boots on the internet for half the price. Your sea boots get a lot of wear, my new boots developed all types of nicks and tears in them .I certainly would not pay £25 again.In winter time I wear thermal socks in my boots which keep the feet and toes toasty warm.

CAPS AND HATS: Most swimmers wear neoprene caps but I found them to be difficult because I have long hair. The first hat cost me 12 pounds and split the second time I wore it. The second cap just kept 'pinging' off my head which was annoying as I had to recover it from the seabed everytime. However I have recently found a very effective hat produced by Speedo purposely for long hair. This hat really works and is comfortable.

I do my own thing and now wear Salty hat. This is a woolly hat rather like a beanie. The first question everyone asks is "Doesn't it become waterlogged?" Well yes it can do but it then tends to trap the water and warms it. I guess doing breaststroke I'm less likely to lose Salty hat because my face is not in and out of the water. But having said that I can still do a mean front crawl and maintain Salty hat. Your hat is also a form of safety to help other sea users spot you. My Mother died at Christmas and I decided to adopt her brightly coloured beanie. Taking her on adventures with me.

I suppose it's what works for the individual. I strongly recommend a hat of sorts for safety, warmth and protection from the sun. But it's the swimmer's choice on make and style. I enjoy my

Salty hat and laugh at the ribbing I get. I've always had a twist of the eccentric.

If you are a distance swimmer--- now here I'm going to define my interputation of the title 'Distance Swimmer' To me a distance swimmer is someone who swims continuously for an hour or more. I'm sure the experts would have something to add to this but hey you can cover a lot of distance in an hour.

I'm always amazed at the swimmers that go into the sea do three strokes and come out again? What is the motivation? All that wetness for such a short time? I've spoken to such swimmers and some said it's the immersion into the cold they enjoy. Others said they like to chat with friends and just swim a little ,while others were completely honest and said it is all they can manage. They have left me in no doubt that

it works for them. Bravo, I'm the first to say each to his own.

PERSONAL BUOYS: If distance is your aim I strongly recommend a personal Buoy. This buoy comes with a belt and sits behind you (well most of the time) It draws other sea users attention to you. For this reason I would always go for the recognised safety colour of electric orange. Orange is universally accepted as a safety warning for the sea. You stand a better chance of a boat or other craft i.e. jet ski seeing the buoy before they see you. I've never had to be rescued (touch wood but more thank you Heavenly Father) but the major problem of sea rescue is actually spotting the person in the water. Even people with kayaks are often impossible to spot in the vast expanse of the sea. So anything that makes you more visible has got to be a good thing.

Also a buoy can be a safety feature ,something to hold onto while you rest. I don't want to be a scare monger here .If you are sensible it's unlikely you will ever need to be rescued but the Sea is the biggest of the big in all this beautiful World so we must broach the subject. Be prepared as the boy scouts say.

When choosing a buoy again shop around. I bought a big tough well-made buoy which cost me £25 BUT after losing it on it's maiden outing I would definitely say put your name and contact details on it in indelible pen checking periodically that it is still clear and bright. I lost my buoy when I foolishly took it off after getting out of the water and laying it beside me. Whooshhh off it flew under the steam of a gust of wind. I knew better than to try to follow it. It was infinitely lighter than me with a good 40 meter start.

Now when you lose a buoy they don't suddenly vanish and if I had had the sense to put my contact details on it would probably have been returned to me. It's also a good idea to put your next of kin contact details on the buoy too. Just a safety measure.

Having lost my buoy on it's maiden outing and learning it's common to do so I question the sense of putting such things as phones, cameras, bank cards etc. inside a buoy.

I personally will not do it but I guess it's up to the individual. So now I needed another buoy as I wouldn't distance swim without one. On the recommendation of Paul, a fellow swimmer, I bought one from E-Bay, brand new for 6 pounds!

Ok it's not as plush as the 25pound one but I actually prefer it.It's lighter and doesn't drag like the big one. It also sits naturally in a better position. But again I wouldn't put anything in it.Never have, never will.

A sea whistle is a must. Worn around the neck it can be useful in many ways i.e. to attract boat users to your presence, or to scare off troublesome wildlife. You might never actually use it but I find it a very reassuring item to have.

You can carry it in your pocket but on a tie around you neck means it's readily available. Lastly it must be a proper sea whistle so it won't rust.

The Swim from Mylor Harbour to Flushing

GOGGLES:

I seldom use goggles. Unlike most distance swimmers, I favour breaststroke as opposed to front crawl. Yes I can do front crawl, rather well actually, not surprising given how long I've been swimming. Also breaststroke is a more difficult stroke to maintain. I regard breaststroke as more revealing of your surroundings and practical to observe the wildlife .

Goggles range in price and styles but generally, they are not overly expensive. Speedo do a brilliant range and are good value for money. Go for comfort and if you are unsure be guided by price. Today you can buy a de-mist spray to clean the goggles but the old-fashioned way of spitting on the lens then rinsing in the sea works just as well.

SEA GLOVES:

My biggest challenge in my wellbeing while swimming are my hands. My middle finger on my left hand is the worst. I don't know why it's never been damaged or sick? The hands can go from chilly ,to cold ,to freezing and finally ice blocks on a long swim.

The sea gloves help but not enough to be comfortable. I've worn gloves inside gloves and again it helps but not a lot. When swimming the Channel swimmers are allowed to use fats to maintain warmth. I experimented first with lard then goose fat before putting my gloves on. It was incredibly messy and really didn't help. Just a tip if you decide to try this for yourself I recommend you put cotton gloves over the fat before you put your sea gloves on, to stop mess.

I found sea mittens on the internet at £38 which was ridiculously expensive but I was desperate so I bought them. I thought perhaps keeping the digits together might be warmer. As the winter chill started to set in I lined the mittens with thermal mittens which keeps my hands 80% warm. But I am always looking for other things to achieve that toastie warm feeling.

Only the other day I tried tin foil as recommended by a fellow swimmer but I think it might have been a wind up as it was totally useless. I am very gullible and trusting.

Some people just bear their ice block hands and feet while swimming then plunge them into hot water at the end of the swim. I remember one day my hands were freezing ice blocks and so painful at the end of a 3 hr swim. There was a workman washing a ventilator in hot soapy water. He went to fetch something and in his absence I plunged my poor hands into the hot water. Ahhhh bliss.

But I do think people making a habit of this hot water remedy could get chilblains or even arthritis later in life.

<u>BREAKING NEWS</u> : Since writing this I think I have solved the freezing hands problem. I've developed a habit of opening and closing my fists during the swim. This helps but if they do get freezing cold I found if I stop and tread water while doing fast windmills with both arms at once the cold freeze in the hands disperses surprisingly quickly. I am so happy to have found this as it makes swimming so much nicer when your hands are warm. Oh just

an afterthought while doing this windmill action you better smile or others might try to rescue you.

Ps.On a more recent swim I decided to splash my arms and hands while going around in a circle. This makes it obvious that I'm doing some weird exercise and not in need of help.

And finally! Now I found if I just change to butterfly stroke the effect is the same but oh so much more stylish. Hooray for warm hands. Phew thank heavens for that.

EAR AND NOSE PLUGS:I never use either of these but some swimmers swear by them. I think the biggest problem is keeping them safe as they are comparatively tiny.They are well engineered and do work. A good investment for a small cost.

This is just some of the gear available for Wild swimming you will have your own ideas but do shop around and do your research. Also keep your ears open, fellow swimmers often give surplus kit away for free. Why? WELL WE ARE JUST NICE OF COURSE.

TECH AND SMART WATCHES: Ah where do I begin? Be very careful with your purchase. Ask around, so many of these smart watches really are not up to what the manufacturers claim. I spent nearly 270 pounds on a Fitbit Iconic which was supposed to be waterproof but it really wasn't. I note the manufactures have now reduced the claim to water resistant. It was useless to me for distance swimming.

.

CHAPTER 4: WIND, WAVES and WEATHER.

One of the things I love and marvel about the sea are the tides.

The thought of those massive volumes of water on the move, not once but twice a day is mind blowing and it helps convince me that there is a God. The moon and gravitational forces control the tides. Tide tables are drawn up the proceeding year and record the time and height of both low and high tide in the morning and afternoon. (please remember that Tide tables are not 100% exact but rather a very good guide) I find the tide table booklets really helpful. There can be as much as 4 to 12 foot difference in the low to the high tide. A spring tide moves the greatest amount of water and has the strongest flow. A neap tide has a gentler flow with less water on the move.

Wind and storm can make a massive difference to the tides even if the storm is far away.

As children we would study the tide tables and there was always great excitement if there was a spring tide which are the biggest of all the tides. We would go to the beach and swim in the big tide loving how far the water was in and covering areas usually visible.

How impressionable are childhood experiences. Even today I love the spring tides.

Swimming with the tide can be a massive help to the distance swimmer.It will carry you along at a rate of knots , swimmers will look for the favourable tides and currents to aid them. By timing your stroke to synchronise with the tide and wave you get maximum propulsion.

A receding tide can be as big a hindrance to the swimmer as a tide which is making is a help.

I remember one day early on in my swimming I was trying to round a headland against the outgoing tide. You can measure your progress in such circumstances by picking a land mark to swim to. This quickly shows you if you are moving forward. This particular day I was not and eventually had to turn around and go with the tide instead. Obviously this can be easily avoided by knowing the movement of the tide before hand.

You can study the wave pattern before each swim. The waves come in patterns or sets and often it's the 5th to 7th wave that is the big one. Before a distance swim I will stand on the water's edge and study the waves and conditions. It's the big wave I'm looking at. Is it a clean wave i.e. it's not breaking in stages before it gets to the shore. What size is it? How strong is it? A normal range of waves is one to 6 foot. We measure the wave from the trough to the crest. So a 6 foot wave is rather like an iceberg, half is above the water level and half below.(an iceberg is one third to two but you get the idea) That's why a wave still has power even once it's broken, the under water force is still there.

From all this i.e. wave ,wind and weather I can assess the risk and suitability for a long swim but please do remember that weather and sea conditions can change at anytime.

Remember, safety first. There's always another day and another swim.

When I do this assessment before a swim I also pray for safety in the water. Not just for myself but for all water users everywhere. So wherever you are know that someone is praying for your safety.

To assess the speed of the wind we have as a guide (nothing is 100%) the Beaufort scale. This is based on observation rather than accurate measurement. It was designed by a Francis Beaufort a naval officer in 1805.It's nice that the scale took the officer's name and even today it is still the most widely used system to measure wind worldwide.

Anything over a force 5- 6. I stay within my depth and treat swimming as a work out with a serious focus on breathing. 6 or over I don't enter the water. The surfers and kite surfers who venture in give amazing ,stunning displays.

I adore swimming in the rain and cheerfully think it makes the water warmer? Here's a tip,when it's raining hard go under the water and swim...... now look up. Impressive sight hey?

Very heavy rain can make the water murky due to any mud washing down from cliffs but it's not serious and perfectly safe to swim in. It's not a good idea to swim in the shadow of a cliff just incase it falls.These falls are often without warning and the debris can cause serious injury.

The cold is a big limiting factor and no amount of layers and fancy gear will totally erase the bitter cold. If the sea temperature is in double figures it's comfortable to swim but once it's dropped down to 6 or7 then it's time to be cautious and limit the length of your swim.

Like all things fashions and techniques have changed in swimming. We have professional divers in the family and they taught me that in order to get into the water you walk up to your waist and wait to acclimatise to the cold. Then they recommend that you duck under to get your body all the same temperature. From experience I can tell you that this method really works and allows you to be comfortable in the water more quickly and enables you to stay in longer. HOWEVER I would definitely be cautious in very cold weather. I remember I got it wrong once and experienced the most excruciating Brain freeze ever. Phew I nearly passed out and this is very dangerous as it can trigger a cardiac arrest. I was OK but it took a good 15minutes to recover and I felt very sorry for myself.

Now days the RNLI recommend a slowly ,slowly approach. It's just common sense and experience. I still use the duck under method of the professionals but am very careful to judge the Temperature first.

The sun can be magnified in the water so remember your sunscreen and a hat. I wear full gear even in the Summer , which covers my limbs guarding against sunburn.

I love the weather's effect on the sea. It would be very limited with out the weather's input.

Here is a bit of a tangent but kind of connected. Be careful of moored boats as they can suddenly swing full circle on their buoy taking you too. The last headland in the photo is called The Stack, an excellent local fishing spot.

Also keep an eye for a boat that is dragging it's mooring. You can tell as it seems to be travelling a ridiculous distance considering it is supposed to be moored.

I had one just the other day and had to spend an extra half hour swimming to keep out of it's way. You can save the owner a lot of hassle if you report it to the Coastguard. But first ask around to see if you can locate the owner. To get to Flushing I have to skirt around Mylor marina .I do this swimming from one moored boat to another being careful not to get too close, I avoid open water as much as I can.This is all a safety strategy.

A moving boat may not notice me in the water but they will automatically avoid moored vessels.

Flushing beach with it's home boats.

Be aware that when any boat is near you in the water it will produce additional waves for you to negotiate. Most boat owners are considerate and will drive the engine slowly as they pass you but occasionally you might get caught in a wave out burst.

Swanpool lake is a bracken mix of salty and fresh water

There is a large colony of water rats at Swanpool lake. If you can forget they are rats they are really rather cute.

CHAPTER 5: There's always another day and another swim.

Since lockdown wild swimming has become enormously popular, even in the Winter. I can remember a few years ago it was just me on the beach in cold weather but the interest and enthusiasm is infectious in this very limited existence we call lockdown.

Also there have developed a huge number of swimming and wellness groups which can provide excellent training, inspiration and swim buddies to share all your adventures with.

These groups are advertised locally or can indeed be found on the beach itself.

I joined a Council backed group run by Nick. I met Nick on Swanpool beach one day and he helped me improve my style as I've never had formal lessons. My style had metomorphesised from my self taught moves as a child. Nick divided the classes into beginners,intermediate and advanced. He gives lessons for each of these groups but is also very happy to do one on one lessons for that extra tailored help.And it's all free. Just 2 personal lessons sorted out my style and allowed me to then go away and practise, practise and more practise.

Swimming is like anything else,the more you do it the better you become.

On every swim I do I spend time paying attention to my style so I don't develop bad habits. It's also important that you breath correctly. That you breath using all your lung capacity and like wise exhaling completely so the lungs are ready for the new fresh air.

On particularly windy days I really indulge my breathing. Concentrating to make the best use of this amazing salty air. I never realised how deep the lungs will breath if given the opportunity. As I practise my breathing I visualise the clean air going down ,swelling and filling the lungs. Equally the spent air with it's cargo of carbon dioxide being expelled. With practise this quality breathing can be done in sync with your swimming strokes adding real power to your steaming forward. Much is said about style and form in swimming. There's even a little snobbery in some comments. I agree it's important to do the most efficient and correct style you can but equally unless you want to become an elite swimmer it's unnecessary to labour the point. I was fascinated and reassured when reading about the requirements for swimming the Channel. When it came to stroke and style the comment was simply 'Whatever works for you'.

If you want a good cold water swimming experience you will automatically improve your stroke ,style and stamina just with practise alone.

I also found that opinions differ depending on who you talk to. So there you have it. If you want to be World class spend all your time in lessons and training but other wise balance it. I think if all the lessons are killing the shear joy of swimming and experiencing the gorgeous sea then it's time to rethink your course and desires.

Ah just a tip, if your club or group organise a social DO go along .It's a time to meet your fellow swimmers and forge bonds .I'm closest to those I met at a beach BBQ and it's nice to put a face to a name.

Safety is the biggest concern when Swimming.

Having the right gear goes a long way towards safety but understanding the water and weather are more essential.When you first start it's a popular choice to swim on a blue flag beach which has lifeguards.

BLUE FLAG BEACHES:

A Blue flag is awarded by the Foundation for the Environment and is an Internationally recognised award.

It identifies and encourages the effort of the local authorities to ensure beaches reach the following criteria.

1.Information about the blue flag must be displayed.

2. Environmental Education must be offered.

3. Bathing water is tested and the result of the test must be displayed. Also the beach must be accessible for the disabled. It must be clean and follow local safety rules.

This award is reviewed annually and can be lost if standards slip.

And most importantly lifeguards and life saving equipment must be available.

Gyllingvase after a heavy storm.

Gyllingvase beach.

And why is it called the Blue Flag Award? Because of the coveted Blue flag which is awarded when standards are met. The photo is of Gyllingvase beach which was named in honour of Henry I son who died in a shipwreck in 1120.

Lifeguard sign on the blue flag beach Gyllingvase.

A Special Thank You:

Here I would like to pause and THANK all those who carry the title of Lifeguard or lifeboat man. Be they full-time or volunteers. You are all heroes, ready to risk your life if necessary in order to safeguard ours . THANK YOU!!

GIVE YOURSELF A FLOATING CHANCE

If you are in trouble in cold water the life guards recommend:

1. Fight your instinct to thrash around.

2. lean back, extend your arms and legs.

3. If necessary gently move your arms and legs to help you float.

4. Float until you can control your breathing.
5. Only then call for help or swim to safety.

Knowing the tidal conditions and weather report are vital when swimming. These are readily available on the web or local radio.

You need to assess the conditions when you arrive to swim. Experience is the best judge of conditions but if you are unsure your friendly lifeguards are always happy to help as well as your fellow swimmers.

The sea is an endless fascination to me with it's patterns of waves and it's dances in the wind. It has so many faces and can be deceptive. It's a foolish swimmer that fails to respect the sea and does not understand when to say NO. Not today. There comes a time when conditions are so rough and unsuitable a wise swimmer will step aside and let the surfers and wind gliders take over. Or change their discipline and go surfing instead.

On such occassions it can be disappointing but I find a bare foot walk across the beach or a long cycle are good alternatives.

It's about being wise, smart and humble. I love watching the surfers and kite surfers. Wow those guys make us distance swimmers look soft in comparism as they fly and jump over and around the massive waves. RESPECT!

I remember one occassion I really wanted to swim despite the raging sea and gale force wind. With the strength of the sea a big shelf (this is a steep drop in the sand of usually 2-4 feet) had formed about 5 foot from the shore. I knew the pull and current would be massive there but I still ventured in, arguing to my cautious self I would be fine once I got out a bit. This was probably true but I was soon in trouble with a massive vicious wave hitting me full on with the force that with time takes cliff faces down. My feet were ripped from beneath me and I went under being turned by the currents and waves as if I was in a washing machine. The force was relentless and I was hit in the face by a stone. I struggled desperately to get my footing and surface again only to be hit by another equally, massive wave. I panicked and thought 'Heck any minute now I will have to be rescued and I'm only 6 foot off the beach'. My body was being battered and I misjudged my breath taking water into my lungs which were screaming for air and safety.

It was the embarrassing thought of having to be rescued so close to the shore that made me draw on that primitive strength within and finally the sea spat me out to the shallows.

I beat a hasty retreat noting that my skin felt like it had been sand blasted and I was sporting cuts, bruises and a bloody nose. OUCH!

When I stripped off my gear I found half a ton (yes no exaggeration) of rough small pebbles that the shear force of the sea had pushed up inside my skin tight gear. Wow what a beast. The sea can be vicious, unrelenting and tempestuous.

ITS'S A FOOL THAT DISRESPECTS THE SEA.

A note of warning too. When on a long swim the sea conditions and weather can change during the course of the swim.The waves can grow and the wind shoot up from a 1or 2 to a 4.or more. Without warning.

 It's good to be aware of this.I have on occassion had to shorten my swim due to worsening conditions.

This is also true if you retrace your swim. Swimming from Gyllingvase to Castle point the wind was behind me on the way there and the waves were doing a grand job of pushing me along. I've learnt to synchinise my stroke with the action of the wave to get maximum propulsion.

However on the way back I was now swimming against the wind and into the waves. Instantly it became twice as hard to make progress. The wind was stinging my face and the waves breaking over me. It was more annoying than scary but it's good to be aware that these things can happen.

It's always a good idea to have a reserve of strength which you can call on if you run into harsher conditions.

However if you find yourself too exhausted and challenged be humble enough to abandon the swim and come to a sooner exit point than planned. You can never beat the sea, it's a massive energy force. Be grateful that you are safe and for the swim you have done.

There's always another day and another swim.

If you are a distance from safety don't panic. Just keep telling yourself that you've got this. With distance swimming it's all about the rhythm of the stroke. It's not about speed though many swimmers can do that too. If you concentrate on the rhythmic stroke and your breathing you will make progress.It might be slow but it will happen. You can also pause and rest holding onto your buoy or hold onto the buoy and kick your feet. This will give you support and some progress.I find it's best not to stop but I've developed an exaggerated doggie paddle,really stretching your arms almost like a wade.This will help relax tired limbs while still making progress.It helps to pick a land mark and determine to get to it. It should be quite close i.e. 200m. Just concentrate on getting there in a slow but progressive swim. Once there choose another and another until you feel safe again.

Just a note, when swimming the Channel or like you have to notify the officials if you intend to change your stroke and must wait for permission to do so.They are keen for the swimmer to maintain the same stroke but will be compassionate to the exhausted swimmer if they only have just a few miles to go. Two remarkable ladies have swum the Channel doing butterfly. Phew that's power .The second lady knocked 6 hrs off the other ladies time. Congratulations to you both. I stand in awe xx

Let's have a break from all the safety.

So today it started to snow? I was excited as I've never swam in the snow before. I didn't have my kit with me so I had a Mermaid moment and swam in my clothes. As soon as I was in the water the snow stopped err.I still had a good swim on the wild side. As I got out it stared to snow again heavily so I rushed back in.......it stopped!

No amount of praying and sweet talking Heavenly Father could produce the desired snow blizzard so I gave up and drove home only for it to really snow during the drive. Not one to give up easily I thought I would swim in the river opposite my house. The snow was falling thick and fast by now. Hooray I thought until I got to the river......the tide was out! Sadly I have to say...I STILL HAVEN'T SWUM IN THE SNOW.

Hooray for our crazy Cornish weather .When we can have all 4 seasons weather in one day. It's perfectly possible to have blazing sunshine in Mylor and torrential rain in Falmouth just 3 miles away.

And Cornish snow, when everything grinds to a holt .Was it waist deep with people being dug out of their cars? Nah 3inches usually does the trick!

If the Cornish weather was a person they would be outrageously eccentric and phaphinagy. But hey we'd love them just the same x x

BOATS AND OTHER CRAFTS When distance swimming you will encounter boats and crafts of assorted shapes and sizes. This can range from a simple kayak to a commercial fishing boat.It's vital to know where the major shipping lanes are and avoid them like the plague. This will stop you coming into the path of the likes such as liners, ferries and commercial container ships etc.

However you will encounter fishing boats, speed boats and small day tripping boats. It's a total nonsense to me that I could buy or rent a small speed boat and without any experience or knowledge take to the sea I'd rather meet a large fishing boat than a day tripper because I know at least the fishing boat will have experienced crew aboard.

If you are unsure of the boats you can skirt the shoreline rather than swim in the open water. This will automatically keep you away from the boats and still give you more or less the same swim.

Castle beach with the Falmouth Hotel on the right.

When a boat comes into my area I assume total responsibility for getting out of the way. I don't relax until I have caught the attention of the skipper and crew so I know they have seen me. You cannot assume that because you are wearing a body buoy the boat will see you. This is not so much lack of care on their part but just how small a swimmer or swimmers can be in the sea. It's a major problem sighting someone in the sea.

So I wave and shout. It's an idea to wear bright gloves and carry a whistle. With care you can get their attention but still be alert and get away as far as possible.

Also look for fishing lines cast out over the side of the boat. Don't want to get tangled up in them.

If all else fails and I can't get the pilots attention or there's a jet ski flying around I will head for the rocks. They might fail to see you but they will instinctively avoid any rocks or shallow water.

When I distance swim I always keep the shoreline in sight so I can reach them fairly promptly if necessary.

Don't ever think to try to out swim a boat. No matter how fast and strong you are the boat will get there first. Also be aware of what is behind you. I remember I hadn't looked behind for a while and was so shocked to see a motor boat slowly following me. I had no idea it was there. Remember to keep a check of what's behind.

Having got a vessels attention then they will almost certainly want to rescue me. I'm amazed at the number of people who automatically assume you need rescuing. I've had boats offer to tow me, kayaks paddling alongside me trying to convince me that I need to allow them to rescue me. I've had people bellow from the shore' are you ok? Have you done this before? Are you aware of the seal beside you?!'.And once a man hung out the window of a very large house and hollered "Shall I call the life boat?!" My fellow swimmers and I do find this frustrating at times but are good humoured about it. Hopefully we will never need such help.

THUNDER and LIGHTNING

If you are swimming and it starts to thunder and lightning you must leave the water immediately. This might involve coming out on the rocks or abrasion platform rather than continue to swim to the distant beach.A 5sec delay between lightning and subsequent thunder means the storm is only a mile away and can get closer in a matter of minutes. As a rule of thumb if the electrical storm is within 5 miles it's important to get out of the water.

I remember very early on in my swimming I was swimming and chatting to a friend when we heard a clamp of thunder. We looked at each other and asked if it was safe to swim in an electrical storm. Neither of us knew but I remember from my physics days salt water is an excellent conductor of electricity so we decided to get out. It must have made an impression because the next time we met a few days later we both had all the answers about swimming in an electrical storm.

This rule applies to everyone including elite swimmers. My hero Martin Strel recounts when he was struck by lightning while swimming. He orated that he was struck out of the river and flew like a plane! He was subsequently unconscious for a few minutes. Just as everyone was concluding he was dead, Martin came too, regrouped and continued to swim!!!

As the author of this book I feel to write next...

DO NOT TRY THIS AT HOME !!!!.

FOG AND SEA MIST I have never encountered serious fog while distance swimming. We don't tend to get a huge amount of regular fog in Cornwall. When we do I would definitely limit my swim close to shore and stay within my depth. You can have a great work out swimming up and down off the shore sometimes for 2 or 3 hours. Concentrating on my style and breathing. It often makes me smile to think what the local seagulls make of this crazy lady who doesn't seem able to make up her mind which way to go. The local wildlife are as curious about us as we are them.

The problem with fog is it can quickly descend and disorientate you.

Sea mist is a different thing to fog. Mist tends to roll in from the horizon giving swimmers plenty of warning. It's often possible to complete your swim by just keeping a wary eye on the impending sea mist. Sea mist seldom comes in as thick as a true fog does.

If a thick fog does descend do not panic but swim parallel to the shore. Work to get within the waveline, this is where the waves tend to gather before travelling to the shoreline approx 7 feet out. Look around for a big land mark such as a pier or a building. You can use them to plot your course . Always work to get within sight of land asap and stay within your depth.

A swimmer should never set off for a distance swim in dense fog.

There is always another day and another swim.

NIGHT SWIMMING.

I have never swam deliberately at night though I did once get caught out swimming in the Mylor creek. I started the swim in late afternoon and darkness descended on the very last stretch of the swim. It was horribly disorientating and really rather spooky. In the end I stopped looking for landmarks and chartered my swim from memory. I know the river extremely well and was able to use details retained in my memory to map my way forward. When I did see a familar boat (this was only when I came upon it) I returned to my memory to work out my course from the boat. My progress was painfully slow. I reminded myself that I was essentially safe, that there is nothing on or in the river to hurt me. With this in mind I was able to relax a little and savour the experience.

Of course the problem was my swim in the dark was unscheduled and I had no equipment to help me. I would never go night swimming on my own. When going with friends I would have 2 torches. A helmet torch for my hat and a big powerful hand torch on a waist cord so I can swim freely.If you don't have a torch stay within your depth.

More marine life tends to come out at night and often the sea is calmer without so many vessels around.

 Night swimming is popular in Cornwall.On full moon nights a lot of skinny dipping goes on. There is nothing like swimming naked but I'd never do so in public or on a distance swim. There's nothing like swimming naked but I do this in privacy and never on a distance swim.On warm early morning swims or beautiful evenings I will take my costume down or off. It's magical and gives me a feeling of oneness with nature. However I want it on record that I would never walk starkers on the beach! Definitely Not my style!!!.

Challenging waters obviously not suitable for swimming.

Carrick Roads. There's been lots of talk of dredging the area in order to make room for bigger luxury cruise ships.

But there's been a lot of opposition because of the rare sea plants and weeds which would be disturbed.

I was on the edge of the shipping lanes one day and was privileged to watch the precise navigation of the massive Viking Venus the cruise ship as she manoeuvred along side an inner wharf of Falmouth docks. I was safe as I was in the shallows of the open sea. It really messed my timing up as I couldn't drag myself away. It was fascinating to see the Venus inch her way around with help from the attendant tugs. 10 out of 10 for all involved. Somehow I don't think I will award myself hero status the next time I squeeze the car into a small space. The bar has definitely been raised!

St Anthony's light house in the distance .As children we used to count the time between the horn blasts as we were falling asleep.

At the entrance to the vast waterway of Falmouth harbour and the Carrick roads are the Manacles rocks and St. Anthony lighthouse was commissioned in 1835 to warn ships of their presence and that of Black rock. In 1987 the keeper was retired and the lighthouse became fully automatic.

Moon lite night over the river.

This is my favourite picture of the sea .God is in control .You might call Him Allah or the Force or

Supreme being but He definitely controls the order of the World.

CHAPTER 6: EVERYONE NEEDS A HERO.

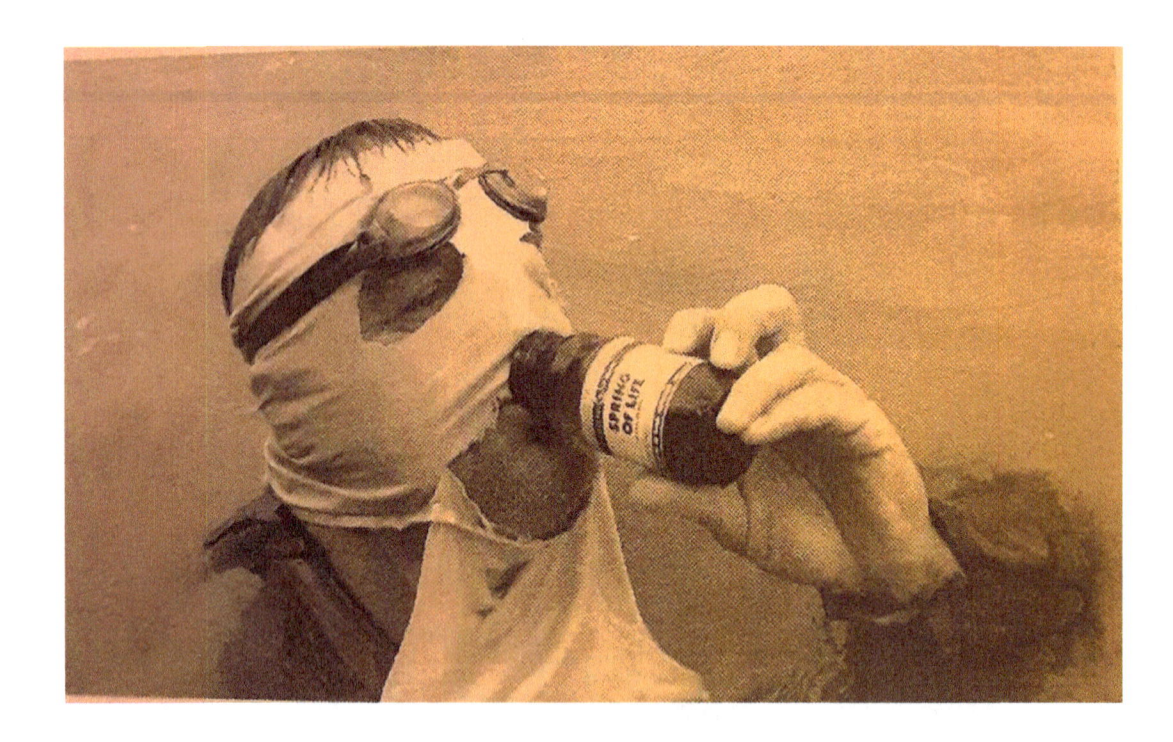

One of Martin's assistants came up with a novel way of protecting his face from the intense sun which was causing such problems with severe sunburn. It's not pretty but it transformed his comfort and well being. Suncream was just not man enough for this job.

In distance swimming my hero definitely is

Martin Strel who has taken distance swimming to a super sonic level. Martin is 62 years old and was born in Solvenia. The medics and experts are baffled by Martin. He is esteemed as being clinically obese and unfit but Martin has developed his own style and is a Marathon Swimmer. He's swam many of the great rivers in the world including the amazing Amazon and will swim for 60 days in a row. He describes himself as part animal part human but his real success is in his ability to push through pain and fatigue. He states the sea has always been a sanctuary for him. As a young boy Martin would take off into the sea to escape his violent Father and his punches.

When Martin started his Marathon swimming he admits he was scared and building stamina was hard with crippling pain and fatigue. He built his swim and mental ability but the real break through came during his swimming of the Danbue he talks of a mighty break through mentally. He notes that something seemed to click within his mind. It allowed him to reach new levels of meditation and mental ability which diminished the pain and fatigue making it possible to sustain such long periods of swimming.

He states that he goes to a different place in his head, he's in 'The Zone' and in a meditative state. Martin will often swim for 15-18hrs a day for 60 days in a row.

The person that observes this effect most clearly in Martin is Matt who mans the support boat during Martin's Marathon swims. Matt says that on his long swims Martin will tell himself stories and notes they often hear a strange gurgling noise as Martin laughs under water.

But Matt quickly interjects that the story telling doesn't really explain what happens in Martin's mind. Martin gives day dreaming a whole new definition. He can spend 10hrs. swimming only 6 feet from Matt's face but be completely oblivious to his presence or his own for that matter. He's really not there but somewhere else, deep in the archives of his mind while still swimming along and moving forward.

Scientists have established that as much as 66% of our brains are sealed and not in use. Could Martin have somehow tapped into a portion of this restricted zone to produce this effect?? This trance like state allows him to push through all pain and human endurance. Do any of us truly appreciate the WOW power and ability within us? We are God's greatest creation and as His children His spiritual DNA courses through our veins. Of course we are extraordinary all of us are.

No other person in the World has ever done this....he is remarkable.

To me Martin epitomises the mystic of distance swimming. He is everything the scientists, athletes and doctors say a person must NOT BE to be a successful distance swimmer. Martin drinks 2 bottles of wine a day even when he swims and eats junk food and is classed as obese. BUT he is an Elite Marathon swimmer. One of his attributes which really helps him is his long lifetime association with the sea. It was his sanctuary from his violent Father and afforded him endless happy watery fun with his friends. The sea was and is Martin's friend. I think this long history of swimming has developed in him a Spiritual bond with the sea. He understands it and has years of experience. He also describes himself as a little crazy, which enables him to think laterally and out of the box. He approaches his mammoth swims with a CAN DO attitude.

Martin says his greatest joy is to be an advocate for Friendship, Peace and Clean Waters.

I SALUTE YOU MY FRIEND AND FELLOW SWIMMER.

Martin's story and experience so inspires me. Not because I want to go swim the Amazon or any major river for that matter but because he confirms to me what I have an understanding of........the strength and capacity of the human mind. I wanted to distance swim but was constantly told you to have to build up to it.

No thought or allowance was made for my long experience in the sea. I was given a swimming assessment and promptly put in the beginners class. I understood this because I had never been taught the correct strokes and technique but after 2 lessons I was conversant with the new style but was still told I wasn't ready to distance swim.

I had a pressing urgency because I have some health problems which are under control but I don't know if this will last forever. I have problems with my back and at times can hardly walk. I don't have time to lounge in the shallows perfecting a stroke.

My arms are too ' heavy and weak' for me to do distance front crawl. I can't consistently lift my arms necessary for distance swimming. To me the solution was easy, just adopt breaststroke but this was frowned on in the swimming world I was encouraged to wait and wait and wait until I built my front crawl.

BUT I am a free spirit and I know what I can and can't do and how precious time is. I knew after a life time of being in the sea how to be safe and the coordinates of my personal ability.

So after just 2 lessons I took off and did my very first distance swim leaving from Swanpool right across the Bay to Castle beach. Yes it was hard, yes it was scary but I did it because I knew I could.

Instead of congratulating me people were sceptical and just warned how dangerous and

foolish I had been. Crazy, the world and his dog were in or on the water that day.

I have since done that swim many times to the point that it's becoming like a quick flit to me. But I recall the enormity of that first time and the sense of safety and achievement I had.

To me we are the authors of our own swim, be it in the shallows or striding forth to distant horizons. Yes we must be very safety conscious and can learn a lot from others but within us are the answers for us personally. We can achieve our goals by doing just as Martin has done by tapping into our inner being.

Martin has put his expertise to good use. Below are his achievements to date.

List of Martins achievements.

1. the Danube   1867miles in58days

2. the Mississippi. 2360 miles in 68 days.

3. the Parana   2484miles in24days

4. the Yangtze   2867miles in40day

5. the Amazon   3273miles in 66 days

Phew, kind of puts my goal of the 28 miles across the Channel into perspective.

They made a documentary about Martin's swim of the Amazon. BIG RIVER MAN. I was surprised how candid it is, definitely a case of warts and all. A truly inspiring watch which is available on You tube.

Respect Martin you are my hero!!

IN THE ZONE.

There has never been as much trust or interest in the Zone or Self ability as there is today. It's recognised that the mind and attitude of a person can be self defining. If you think you can or you can't you are probably right. I have found this to be invaluable when applied in Wild and distance Swimming.

Issues like cold, fatigue, edgy fear etc. (you can add you own issues) can all be helped by being in the Zone. Before a long swim I will spend time loading with calories, getting a good sleep and preparing my thoughts with yoga and meditation or simply just pondering the swim. I keep this all positive and enlightening. Dealing with fear is liberating. e.g. when Sammy suddenly appears at my shoulder it can really spook me but I have learnt to disassociate or not own these thoughts. If they come into my mind I just chase them away and replace them with positives. e.g. It's recognised that 99% of Cornish Marine life is harmless and it's unlikely you will ever meet the 1%.

My Mother always quoted an old Jewish proverb 'Trouble will come but that doesn't mean you have to draw it up a seat'. By dwelling on your fears you emphasize their potential so block them. Wild swimming is an edgy sport ,that's what makes it so enlivening.

The cold a swimmer experiences is a bigger issue to some than others. Again your mind-set can have a massive impact on the degree of cold you experience. Now I'm not talking about wishful thinking or advocating that you do not heed what your body communicates to you but just as a cheerful heart produces a happier day so positive vibes can help the mental insulation of your body whilst swimming.

For more information and a greater expansive thought on this turn to:

THE ICEMAN: (SEE HIM ON YOU TUBE)

IF we can learn a % of this it is really going to help our swim.

The Ice man:

Wim Hof, better known as the Iceman for his extraordinary ability to endure the cold. He swims long distances in Antarctica and is involved in extensive research on the extremes the body can take given the right training. I have studied some of Wim's teachings and participated with him on courses. It's fascinating and has caused me to aim to swim in Antarctica in the not so distant future. Burrr.

Gratitude:

Another wonderful tool in life is the healing and enjoyment of expressing Gratitude. This discipline can have fast acting and long lasting joy in our lives. When swimming I always take the time to say thank you. I'm thanking a Father in Heaven but you might have your own idea, maybe the Universe etc. Gratitude is so powerful and can change the way we view the World and our position in it.

So what does this have to do with swimming? Well that depends on you and your acceptance of the principal and practise of expressing gratitude. I have found that a grateful heart is a precious tool in life. A grateful society would have no hate,rascism,violence and all the other horrids of sickness in the World today. If you approach swimming just as physical exercise you will get fit but I hope you will also strive to experience your place in the water and your relationship/understanding of the sea and indeed in the World other than what you experience in regular life. TRY it. I guarantee you will wind up smiling. Reel off ALL THAT YOU ARE GRATEFUL FOR XX Your swimming will be a stronger, deeper experience which over time will deepen you.x

<u>ASSESS YOUR SWIM</u> At the end of a distance swim I always take time to savour the experience. How it made me feel, was my style consistent, am I cold /tired- by what %? What did I see on the swim, wildlife, wave pattern, weather change?

In life I often rate experiences out of 10 and my swimming is not an exception. If I have experienced a problem I later analyse it and determine how I could avoid it in another swim. I'm a very pragmatic person and when necessary shrug my shoulders and determine that BAD HAPPENS. This is also possible in swimming and just to shrug my shoulders and say THERES ALWAYS ANOTHER DAY AND ANOTHER SWIM can be healing in itself. No regrets or recriminations just learn from the experience and MOVE ON.

TAKE A BREAK: We all know the expression 'Too much of a good thing……is too much'

I love my swimming and rejoice in the wonder of waterways, lakes, rivers and the sea most of all BUT I don't want it to take over my life so there's no time for all the other lovelies that I rejoice in e.g. music, reading, travelling etc. Because of this I balance my activities so nothing starts monopolising my time.

I also am cool about taking time out from any sport or interest. March is esteemed to be the coldest month of the year to swim so I will often take a break coming back at around Easter time depending on when it is placed in the year. I find this refreshing and revitalising. Don't get so hung up with the brag of swimming all year round that you find yourself not enjoying your swimming quite so much. After all you know what they say

A CHANGE IS AS GOOD AS A REST X

A red sky at night is a sure sign of good weather.

The docks and Pendennis Super Yacht yard as seen from Flushing beach

The Pendennis Super Yacht yard is Internationally renowned and we often see the most beautiful Super yachts visiting for repairs or maintenance work. They add a very glamorous look to the harbour.

St Mawes Castle which sits opposite Famouth castle.

CHAPTER 7 . HEALTH AND WELL BEING

There are important things to know about your health when distance swimming and simple tips can save a lot of grief and pain.

Rubbing and Chafes .

Something that seldom gets mentioned when you are new to distance swimming is rubbing and chafing of garments against skin when swimming. First I knew about this was when I completed a 3hr. swim in my early days. I was totally unaware of my injury in the cold water But, was horrified when I stripped off my kit only to find deep cuts and rubs under my arms. My whole underarms were ablaze with raw skin and the joint of the arms had deep cuts.I couldn't believe the damage, bearing in mind it was only wet fabric against skin,I hadn't been attacked with a knife or by a sea creature.

Once out of the water the wounds scream pain. OUCH with a capital O!! It's important to attend and care for these areas of damage as they can become easily infected. I found Germoline to be the most effective treatment but that's no surprise as at our house it's the ultimate wonder cream. This comes from Mother who told a story of a Service man in a prison camp. He had an ulcerated leg and only half a tube of Germoline to treat it. With careful ,sparing use it saved his leg.

We were raised with Germoline. Every scrap, cut, bump and bruise was carefully anointed with Germoline. Even the cat had his wounds

treated with Germoline. It's old fashioned but effective and readily available.

A badly chaffed armpit will take at least 2-3 weeks to heal but it's so simple to avoid. Just like marathon runners all vulnerable areas need a generous thick layer of Vaseline to be protected. Under the arms and especially where the arms join the torso and around the groin area. These are the obvious sites but there maybe other areas for individual swimmers.I have an oval area at the top of one leg that will arbitrarily rub if not vaselined.This problem is so easily avoided, ignore it at your peril. The problem can be so severe swimmers have elected to swim bare chested on very lengthy swims.

SEA SICKNESS IN SWIMMERS. In 1993 I had a car accident which resulted in a nasty head injury. This caused alterations in my body and my perception of the World. One notable change is my strange concept of motion. My body takes exception at any change in motion resulting in horrendous motion sickness. To my dismay I found I was experiencing sea sickness while swimming. How weird is that? But the sea can have strange effects on some. My brother Peter was a deep sea fisherman and would suffer terrible nose bleeds if working in the North sea, but only ever in the North sea? I couldn't believe my seasickness but I discovered later on that sea sickness is a common aliment for distance swimmers. I find it's especially true when the waves are bouncy but not huge. The rhythm of the sea waves can interfere with the swimmers concept of motion and can actually cause the swimmer to vomit.YUK.

I can't think of anything more horrid but I have noticed things that I do to stop it.

1.Periodically close your eyes. This will stop the mesmerising action of vision/motion.

2.Gently turn your head from side to side. Again breaking that pattern and relieving any tension or fatigue developed from the constant swim.

3. Sing, doesn't matter how badly. As a distraction singing is magic. I honestly believe there's an element of total focus and repetition in your swim which determines the extent of the seasickness. I say this knowing I am possibly in the highest bracket of maximum motion sickness. You name it, I get it to maximum effect I've been in the care of stewards and doctors I've been so bad. I even had to give up paddle boarding because it made me seasick. So I sing loud, sing funny this will distract your focus and ease/relieve symptoms.

4. some people recommend a barley sugar.

5. I never eat anything while on a distance swim. I can almost hear the medics shouting their protest, I concede eating and drinking might work for others but not for me. The very thought makes me gag.

However I do calorie stack like the Marathon Runners. The night before the swim I have a wonderful time (I adore food) building a reservoir of carbs, protein, fats and plenty of fluids. I find this really works for me. Before the swim I will eat a banana, a handful of nuts and a pint of water. On longer swims say 4hrs + food and liquid during the swim would be essential. It's my goal to swim the English Channel. For such a lengthy swim I would take medical advice about motion sickness medication.

Having said all this I'm happy to say motion sickness doesn't affect every swimmer or most people all the time. I do wish someone would have mentioned it to me though. The first I knew about it was while I was swimming in the open sea on the way to Mylor Harbour. I really suffered that day.

<u>GLUE EAR</u> .Maybe like I was, you have heard of this expression but are a little unsure of what it is.

Glue ear happens when the empty middle ear canal fills up with fluid. This can cause temporary hearing loss and at times an infection can develop but it generally clears up in 3 months. This can affect both ears. Surfers tend to suffer from it. I know in the 70s they used to put grommets in to help drain the channel but I've not heard of it been done for a while. I get periodic pain from glue ear but in Winter it's much better as I'm not covering the great distances due to the cold. I've experienced about a 6/10 pain with it and just a shadow of hearing loss. I always take care to dry my ears well turning my head to each side to let any water drain out. Ear plugs can be a big help to protect the ear canal. They are cheap ,well engineered and yes you can still hear while wearing them.

EXITING THE WATER AFTER A LONG SWIM

Getting out of the water after a distance swim can be challenging. I am always quite wobbly and unable to stand immediately .To come to a vertical standing position from being a length of time on your stomach horizontal to the water requires an adjustment to your sense of motion.

I'm sure many swimmers just stride James Bond style out of the water but I know I'm not alone in being unbalanced as other swimmers have told me so. As well as balance problems you can also feel vaguely sick but it's nothing serious just a combination of motion and over exertion in the swim. (quite a different feeling to early stage hypothermia.)

Not wanting to appear drunk and disorderly as I leave the water I have learnt to take my time. I slow down as I'm coming to the end of my swim and just relax, slowly making my way to the shore. The rescue brigade often show up here convinced that I definitely need rescuing today. I politely decline and explain I'm just acclimatising to the water.

If the tide is coming in you can use the incoming waves to gently carry you. I remember once at Castle beach the waves were getting bigger and bigger. I was literally lifted up and swept in the arms of each wave. I knew that although the waves were not very forceful I mustn't look behind me to see the size of them. Eek very edgy.

Castle beach is difficult to come into as it is basically all abrasion platform in the water.(i.e. rock shelf). This is fine if the tide is in and I would always choose to swim in a foot of water using my hands to walk on if necessary rather than try to negotiate the slippery rocks in a motion drunk wobbly way. It's safer and if you take your time you should reach the beach with your dignity in tact.

BEWARE OF LOOSE FLOATING WEED.

Be wary of seaweed floating loosely on the surface of the sea. I never realised how much loose weed there is cast adrift and at the will of the tides. I always swim away or around it. Never swim into it because what often looks like a small area of weed can be hiding an iceberg effect with great heavier clumps floating beneath it.

I've heard of swimmers getting tangled in loose weed up to their necks. Very difficult, even with the help of your fellow swimmers it's drastically difficult to escape while in deep water. Definitely swim around and away from it.

TIME OF REFLECTION.

AS I swim I really wallow in the absolute joy of the Environment. It's a time to study the sea, the surroundings and the wild life. As well as a perfect time to reflect on life generally and maybe figure out something or just see where to go.

The sea is also the perfect place to vent your anxieties privately.

One day the wind was up and the waves were smallish but clean. (this means they are not breaking randomly or before they reach the shore.)

I was totally stressed out and miserable. I didn't want to swim but I know from experience if you push yourself through that feeling it will be good and make you feel better. As I was gently swimming a feeling of deep sadness overcame me and I started to cry and cry. Crying turned to bawling and bawling to breaking my heart. I had received some unjustified criticism at the weekend and it tipped me over the edge. All the sadness of Mother's death at Christmas came flooding out and all the deeply buried worries that I hadn't really dealt with. The sea was rocking me gently wrapping me around in the natural environment. It was like a pressure cooker release in the depths of Nature. I'm from Italian stock so I can cry freely and understand the valuable, creative safety valve of a good cry.

Sure enough after a while I did start to feel better. I can recommend the sea as a great environment and place to go to release such emotions, be it that you cry, shout or thrash around whatever works for you. I compare going to the sea to spill your emotions to burying your face in the fur or neck of a much loved pet. They both make wonderful passive listeners.

After this release I felt better and was able to examine the sadness objectively and in a positive prayerful way. I walked out of the sea renewed.

PEACE WAS RESTORED

Before I get out of the water I have found that if I bounce up and down with vigour it quickly warms the body and hands. I also do some exercises such as waist twists, raising knees and butterfly stroke which is a work out all in itself . Pausing before I leave the water and doing cardio exercises has made all the difference to my post swim time. It allows me to leave the water comfortably warm and no longer am I struck not being able to negotiate zips ,buttons etc.

HYPOTHERMIA I was shocked to learn that it's possible to suffer hypothermia AFTER a swim. It's made me very aware of the condition of my body during a swim. Before swimming I will have a handful of nuts and a banana and a good drink of water an hour before I swim.This gives the body something to work with along with the food I ate the night before.

SAFETY ALWAYS COMES FIRST.

So if I feel a chill creeping in I will swim faster or stop and bounce in the water. But if the cold becomes a problem or if I were to start to shiver I will always get out and get warm calling it a day.

Remember there's always another day and another swim. Safety must come first.

One thing I did learn by experience is the importance of regular swimming to adapt and keep tuned to the water temperature. I tend to swim every other day because much as I love swimming I don't want it to monopolise my life. I will swim 1 or 2 long distance swims a week as I need time to recover after a long swim. I also favour early swimming. I like to be out at the crack of dawn and get some good distance before the World wakes up. There's something spiritual about being in the water as the sun rises and I never get over the sense of privilege it is to be there. By swimming regularly it gives the body a chance to regulate to the ambient temperature. The importance and reality of this was brought home to me in December. My Mother was very ill and sadly died after a short illness. During this time I didn't swim for weeks and weeks. When I finally returned to the sea I couldn't believe how FREEZING cold it was. I have never known it to be cold like that either before or since.It was simply my body had not acclimatized to the cold over my weeks not swimming. It took me a week of 3 or 4 swims to get back to a more manageable cold.

Hypothermia is always a concern and I think if a swimmer starts to shiver during a swim you have to take this very seriously and get out of the water asap. Shivering can be a real alarm bell. Wearing a cap or hat can save as much as 20% heat loss.

Prior to a swim you can go for a quick run, do some stretching or my favourite....just bounce. All of these make for a more comfortable entrance into the water.

Of course Hypothermia affects people differently but a mild case will show symptoms of shivering, bluish skin but the swimmer will still be conscious. In cases like this the swimmer must leave the water, get out of their wet gear quickly and have something warm to drink. A gentle exercise will help, like jogging on the spot and doing some arm turns. They should recover relatively quickly but should not be left alone and be kept warm.

The next stage of hypothermia is concerning and the swimmer although conscious is in need of assessment. The life guards are well trained to spot serious hypothermia.In a moderate case the swimmer might be really shivering, have difficulty speaking or answering questions. Their eyes will be dilated and their skin will be very gray.They need to be taken to the medical bay and be in the care of a first aider who will assess if they need further help.

In severe hypothermia the body doesn't shiver but it is very clear the swimmer is in need of emergency help and 999 should be called without delay. They might be unconscious, very white and unable to recognise others or communicate. Their body can also go rigid.

All these stages need careful attention to stop the hypothermia escalating. If emergency help is not immediate then it's good to get the patient out of their wet gear and cover them with as much warm, dry clothing as possible. It helps for another to lie down with them in a full body hug to hopefully transfer warmth person to person. But don't despair a 999 call for extreme hypothermia will be dealt with swiftly.

It's vital not to ignore the early signs of hypothermia or it will develop further and surprisingly quickly.

After a swim it's important to get out of your wet clothes asap. Dry Robes which are changing coats are hugely popular at this time. They cost about £130 or £150 if you want long sleeves.I've never met anyone who isn't totally in love with their dry robe despite the expense. Given the opportunity they will endlessly pontificate about the robe's qualities and 100% recommend that you get one. A very successful product,effective in it's duties and lives up to the manufactures promises. It also comes in a rainbow of colours.

BUT, I didn't buy one. This was simply because I usually cycle to my swim and leave my bike chained up for long hours while I swim. I worried that it might well be too big a temptation for someone to find a Dry Robe unattended for so long.

Looking on the web I found a myriad of alternative makes at various prices and settled for one that costs £40. It looks like a Dry robe ,is well made and perfectly suitable. It does lack street cred as it doesn't have any logo.

Will I ever buy a dry robe?I wouldn't rule it out,it is a wonderful product.

Recently I also discovered Speedo water wear. It's very well made and beautiful quality And their costumes stay on in rough surf! Speedo also do changing robes. Check it out their prices are reasonable too.

It helps to have a hot drink after a swim. I make a special cake which is adapted from an old fruit cake recipe that Muriel my sister's Mother-in-law used to make. I've taken out all the sugar and butter and use a twist of olive oil and a dessert spoon of honey instead. It's rich and full of the goodness of nuts ,mixed fruit, whole cherries, coconut, seeds and wholemeal flour. The recipe is very good natured and never goes wrong. Really, even the cat could make it. If you have any left overs in the fridge like stewed apple, bit cream or custard just put it in the cake.It's really good for you and you only need a little to satisfy and it's appreciated by your fellow swimmers. ENJOY X.

Muriel's Rich Fruitcake.

5oz Butter

5oz sugar

2 Eggs

8oz White Self Raising Flour

8oz Mixed Fruit

1/4ptmilk

Swimmer's Cake

Leave out the butter and sugar

10oz Wholemeal Flour

12oz Mixed Fruit

8oz Mixed Nuts

4oz Whole Cherries

1/3 Pint Milk (any)

4 tsp Baking Powder

A twist of oil and honey.

☆don't forget the baking powder or the cake will be flat as a pancake due to the wholemeal flour. Just mix it all together and put in a moderate oven 160 and cook till knife comes out clean when you spear it. ENJOY! X

Cramp

If I ever get cramp it will always be in my right lower leg. From my biology days I can tell you it is my R. gastrocnemius. He gets very bolshy and will crunch up with no warning. Cramp on land is not serious but when you are in very deep water it can be challenging. It's no good trying to swim through it so I suggest you float for life as our heroes the lifeguards say. And relax, and relax again. You can use your mind to relax the offending muscle by thinking of happier things i.e. the beauty all around you. Massage is helpful. Eventually in your stillness the offending muscle

WILL relax. Just a warning, move off slowly or the muscle might well crunch again. He needs to know that his protest is noted and due consideration has been given.

JUST TALK TO THE CREATURES.

This might seem a little off beat, even radical but I've been involved with cat rescue all my adult life and have come to appreciate that animals have a lot more insight than we give them credit for. So I would definitely advocate talking to the seal who pops up next to you.

This instantly clarifies that you are not a trespassing seal (bearing in mind most distant swimmers are dressed in black) and puts you in the natural order of life and the food chain.

We must be intelligent and responsible towards the creatures. It might seem like a good idea to try to smooth or God forbid ride a seal or feed a creature but this could result in serious injury. To you not them. Remember they are in their natural habitat and if anyone is going to get hurt it Will be you. Also you have a responsibility to your fellow swimmers to treat everything about the water with reverence and respect. Just suppose you get lucky and manage to feed the seal without harm but how would you feel if the next swimmer gets bitten because they don't have any food? But hey you are smart enough to know this.....AREN'T YOU???.

<u>JELLY FISH</u> A troublesome problem to the swimmer is jellyfish. A bloom of jellyfish can be difficult to negotiate around. Their sting comes from their long tentacles and can range from being painful to life threatening to anyone with allergies .They are beautiful to watch as they swim but from a distance. At times the sea can fill with massive blooms and I will find an alternative beach to swim or the river. I've never been stung and I'm touching wood as I say this but I've had anaphalytic shock from wasp stings. It's just not worth the risk.

Another equally nasty little species is the weaver fish who stings if you are unfortunate enough to stand on one at the waters edge. If you see a swimmer suddenly jump up and scream in agony it's probably due to a weaver sting. Wearing sea boots can help to protect your feet in this situation. Both these species deserve the title of Nasty little beasties! The stings require medical attention but in the meantime treating with hot water and vinegar is effective.

Writing all this about safety and well being I want to balance it by saying that with care you will be fine. But as with any edgy sport safety has to be an absolute priority.

If you are wise, well prepared and humble enough to say 'um I don't think I can do this or the weather is changing I better leave the water or burr Im getting cold/tired I better get out etc. you will be safe.

Remember there is always another day and another swim and it's a wise, cool person who is humble enough to call it.

CHAPTER 8: A SWIMMER'S BLOG .

In writing this blog I really hope the reader can experience a flavour of Wild swimming. I keep the log to capture the feel of excitement and satisfaction of a swim well swum.

Flushing beach with it's large quay.

It's best to do this sooner rather than later , while the memory is fresh. I always write a short description of the swim. The feel ,thoughts and sightings of the day. It's so wonderful to read at a later time.

I find reading my blog can project me right back to the day and I can feel the experiences of that swim.

A lot of swimmers take a camera with them and return with the most amazing pictures. I am a dreadful photographer but I do plan to change this.

This chapter has some examples of my blog and reflections I hope you enjoy my slant on distance swimming.

MY VERY FIRST DISTANCE SWIM.

Breaking News!! Today I did my first distance swim. I went in at Swanpool and spent time wondering if I should go but eventually after a big prayer for safety I set off.

The headland around to Gyllingvase seemed very lonely with no houses or walkers that I could see from the water.

Now days I can flit from Swanpool to Gyllingvase no problem. But that first swim was very edgy but thrilling at the same time. The sea scares me, she dares me.

The water was crystal clear with just a small wave. And it was warm, so warm. I was nervous that I might meet Nibbles the seal who hangs around this area. Nibbles is a small lone seal and delights in nibbling swimmer's feet.

Ugh just what I don't need on my first distance swim. It was also the first time that I used my modified swimming style as taught by Nick the instructor. I was very disciplined in maintaining the new style and was surprised how easily I adapted from my personal self-taught style of many years. But it wasn't hugely different.

I'm confident that my own style would have delivered me there too.

The way around the cove seemed long and I didn't arrive at the land points as quickly as I imagined I would but I kept my focus on the feel and enjoyment of the swim.

One thing I adore about the sea is it supports you totally. In the deep there is no chance of tripping or falling over. The sea is magnanimous in it's work on your behalf. I found if I synchronised my stroke with the wave I would glide delightfully along with the sea's assistance.

At one point I had a little panic but was quickly distracted by a cormorant who had joined me and was ducking and diving ,gliding around me. Almost to say " This is how you do it"

Since that very first distance swim I've noticed that cormorants are very often around swimmers. It makes me wonder why? Is it coincidence, curiosity or do we some how stir the fish up as we move thus making us ideal companions?

Cormorants are credited for eating pounds of fish a day.

Phew that's a lot of fish which makes me excited to realise there must be a good fish supply in our local waters to sustain this.

I guess we will never know why the cormorants are so keen to seek the swimmers out but I like the idea that we help them fish....so I will go for this reason.

Finally Gyllingvase beach came into view and I felt excited and refreshed at the same time. I was getting there with no mishaps along the way. On this side of Gyllingvase beach there's an unhelpful rip current. It's not a huge rip but with the tide now going out I found it very hard work to get through. In fact I had to change course and cut across it at 90 degrees. I was thrilled to see fish jumping around me. It was beautiful to watch and made me wonder if it was their answer to the rip as their jumping followed the diagonal as well.

I was so excited to reach Gyllingvase beach I had done my first distance swim. I wasn't exhausted or cold and just stayed in the water practising my front crawl.

The water was so refreshing and I felt that I had been lucky to experience the natural dimension of this world where the sea is boss

and residents move politely around the area. Such unspoken beauty was felt as well as seen and all my senses were awakened. I've never felt so alive.

And then, quite unexpectantly I experienced a Forest Gump moment and started to move off again, across the expanse of Gyllingvase beach and headed for Castle beach. This is the next beach along and would mean I had swam right across Falmouth Bay.I felt so much more confident and relaxed. It's a more open expanse of water with lots of people around both on the beach and in the sea.

I was soon at Castle beach having swam a distance of 3miles. I was so happy and proud of myself. Just as I came into Castle Beach a seal's tail popped up in front of me. Wow did Nibbles swim all the way with me? Who knows but I was thrilled to see her and also pleased that she had not made her presence known earlier in the swim.

I did think to swim back to Swanpool but decided to err on the side of caution and finish my swim at Castle. Castle beach is very long and spread out so I determined that the shop would be the official point as it's about middle of the beach. But I suppose you could claim victory a good ten minutes earlier, its a long beach!

BOUNCY WATERS.

Gosh it was bouncy at Gyllingvase this morning but nice and warm. I went in with 2 friends and got pushed around by the waves. Not the day for any distance so we retired to the beach and had the yummiest bacon roll and a wonderful marathon chat.

BURRR IT WAS COLD.

Today it was cold but I think it was more the atmosphere . I swam for a couple of hours and was comfortable until I got out. Burr it was cold.

I was just grateful I had the car with me. I raced home and showered then put on as many clothes as I could. A couple of cats came to welcome me so I put one under each arm. Then I went to check on Mummy. She was all warm and snug so I stuck my feet under the blankets

as we chatted. Mother is not one to suffer in silence and I was quickly told to take my ice blocks (feet) elsewhere.

Phew I thought this Winter swimming was going to be a stinch but now I'm not only planning thermals for tomorrow's swim but I bought a thicker set this afternoon. Holy Molie it was COLD!

WOW WHAT AN EXPERIENCE:

Today I had the most surreal experience on a distance swim. I was about 300m from the shore when I came across a shelf of rock. This allowed me to walk with water lapping at my feet. I was totally surrounded by water and the only shore was far away. Wow what an amazing experience. It made me think of Peter when he walked to the

Saviour on the water. What faith it must have taken to take that first step.

Nature is often producing these marvellous fleeting experiences. Which I was reminded of when I walked off the edge of the shelf...SPLASH!

GORGEOUS WARM WATERS.

Excuse me, excuse me ? Did I miss something ? I know I have a reputation for mammoth naps due to a nasty head injury but I'm wondering if I slumbered through Winter and have woken up in Spring?

It was truly gorgeous in the water today. I kept questioning if I would ever need my thermals.

So I just kept going right across the Bay to Castle beach and back to Gyllingvase where to my delight I saw Nick the instructor and Paul a fellow swimmer. Always fun to have a good natter. OH happy day.

<u>EEr AHH PHEW!!! WHAT A DAY!.</u> I set off on my swim of Mylor Creek to Mylor Harbour. It was just cracking light. I saw a seagull fight with a heron. No serious damage on either side but I'd love to know what it was about.

When I reached the harbour, it was bouncy which gave me a really good work out I swam to the far side of Mylor beach BUT as I neared the open sea I knew instantly I mustn't proceed and go around the headland. The oyster boats were lurching and really riding the waves ABOUT TURN FOR ME!

I thought I would just swim back up the river but now the tide was going out. Swimming against the tide which is coming through a narrow channel is not for the weak hearted. The now boisterous waves were breaking over my head and my previously well behaved buoy kept coming into my face. What a crazy work out but after an hour and half of swimming against the tide I was exhausted so decided to call it a day and hit land. That was hard work and required going through thick weed. Mylor beach may produce World Champions but it's horrid for swimming. By the time I got to shore I felt I had been through the mangle and had the prospect of a long walk home. I was packing up when a sudden gust took my new buoy. I knew not to follow it and had to watch £25 disappear over the waves.

On my long walk home one of the old ladies gave me some cat food as her kitty had died. I am known in the village for my cat rescue efforts. Love cats.

SURPRISE the old lady emerged with a ton and a half of cat food. Declining was not an option.

So I'm cold, been through the wringer and carrying a mountain of cat food. OH happy days xx

Swanpool once again. Sorry but I love this beach xx

Swanpool Lake. Lynyeyn Pryskelow in Cornish. There was formerly a silver mine beneath the lake. It is 150m deep and produced a rich return of silver/lead ore. It was closed in 1865 but reopened at a later date only to close forever a few years later.

Swanpool lake with the old crazy golf site in front. We had so much fun as children trying to master the art of crazy golf.

Study the pattern in the sea photo below.

FAMILY PICTURE: So you see it's not surprising I'm a water and beach enthusiast .It's in my genes. The other little girl in the photo is my sister but she takes after the English side of the family whereas I am from the Italian stock .

My early beach days.

BLUSTERY DAY.

The sea today was like a washing machine cycle. The waves although little were criss/crossing the shoreline making for breaks and splashes in the face. Because I didn't have my gear my hands and feet were bare. It's so nice to swim without gloves or boots ,so liberating and free. But it does limit the time you can swim as they quickly become first mildly cold, then freezing,then numb and finally ice blocks. At ice block stage it's not as painful but it's an indication that the body is becoming seriously cold so when this happened I swam to the shore bounced up and down in the water to warm and then got out.

INDIAN SUMMER.

Ah what a day. It was truly beautiful on the seafront today. More like July than late November.

I had a fabulous swim from Castle to Gyllingvase and back again. The water is still warm which is surprising. But alas there was one sad incident today......I lost my salty hat. She must have slipped off as I was doing front crawl. It seems my lot that the sea will acquire my goodies one by one.

A fellow swimmer read this and sent the oh so helpful advice...

Be care that your clothes are well fastened!!

19th Nov.

Gosh what a day. This morning it was raining and blowing a mini hooli.This afternoon here in Mylor we have sunshine and stillness. ! I was out at the crack of dawn first swimming the Mylor Creek and then enjoying the bluster of the sea at Flushing. For me there is just no competition to the sea from the river. I like to be out early. It sets you up for the day and doesn't monopolise all your time. Happy swimming everyone.xxx

<u>A ROYAL ESCORT.</u>Today I swam the river and back again.The tide was going out on the way home and I could see how much stronger I am now. It was just turning dusk on the way back which

flooded the scene in a warm glow. The big houses on the shore had their lights on making everything look magical and dare I say it, somewhat Christmassy. I am friends with the resident swans, they visit my home and I give them good nutritious tasties. So imagine my joy when they joined me on my swim home. Talk about a Royal escort.

22/11.

So new week coming up thank goodness. I've been laid up with my back again so no swimming for a day or 2 it's annoying. But tomorrow is the day Hooray. I have a fab new Salty hat, like to see the wind blow this beasty off. And sea mittens which come with a warmth guarantee .I will hold them to it..Happy swimming everyone xx

MY WELCOMING COMMITTEE.

Oh what a joy. Perfect conditions to swim from Flushing to Mylor in just an hour and half. I was genuinely surprised how warm the water still is. A peaceful, joyful day. There always seems to be the same heron to welcome me at the end of the swim. He really watches me intently.

But today I made a mistake, I wished him good morning. There he was gone! I spooked him. I hope it doesn't put him off welcoming duties xxx

SLAYING MY DRAGON.

What a fantastic day a real bonus. Today I slayed the Dragon! I swam around Pendennis point. Probably the trickiest part of my distance swim. Phew it's not for the faint hearted. It scared me, it dared me. I felt challenged and had to swim hard to get around. But I was never in any danger.

I remember when I was young, as a family we would snorkel in the lee of the Point but it was drummed into us Never go round the Point. Fast forward to my sailing days as a young woman and memories of some very fast tacking to round the point safely comes to mind. But hey the dragon is slain. I always rate things out of 10 and in my opinion I'd say the Point is a 7 out of 10. The deep respect and trepidation about swimming around Castle Point proves the power of a parents words. It was drummed into me that a combination of tides and cross currents makes the Point a very tricky stretch of water to negotiate. Others who haven't been indoctrinated by their parents probably think this is a gross exaggeration and unnecessary. However as many of my family are professional divers I stand by my Beast of the water description!!

I survived and in celebration I swam right across the Bay to Swanpool which was pure joy. Such a gorgeous ,gorgeous day. Thank you Heavenly Father. PS no sign of Nibbles.

PULLING IT TOGETHER. Today I swam from Flushing beach to Swanpool to Gyllingvase . This is 2 sections of my swim route combined and just over half of my charity swim for MND. It's the first time I have combined 2 sections. It was hard but not as hard as it could have been.

The Flushing side of the swim was a milpool and then I came to Castle Point, which was it's usual angry self.

Middle of Summer? Not at all it was February.

MISCHIEF: It's my observation that some creatures have a sense of fun and even mischief. I saw this in the Canadian geese today.

I was swimming in the creek when a 5 strong formation of Canadian geese suddenly came flying straight at me. Usually it would not be a problem and I would just duck under the water BUT...I never put my head in the river just incase it has some resident germs. In a split second I had to chose between germs or being duck dived by the geese. A bit of a blow on the head or a poke in the eye. I decided to take my chances with the birds, saying a silent prayer whilst wondering how much this was going to hurt. Canadian geese are big birds. Ok here they came 6,5,4,3,2 wishhhh.The ring leader just skimmed my crown I could feel the wing action but he never actually hit me. I'd just been spoofed by a flock of geese! As they passed me they all let out a shriek of delight and whooping I still marvel when I think about it.Hooligans!

Another time in the river I met the resident male swan. It was mating season and as he saw me he went into full aggressive stance. He skimmed across the water with his wings wide open towards me. Now I know the resident swans they visit me for treats.As soon as I spoke to the male he recognised my voice and was instantly embarrassed by his stance I was touched by his 'almost apology 'while also being relieved that I wouldn't have my first duel with a male swan today. Phew.Creatures have greater faculties and characters than we give them credit.

REASONS WHY I DISTANCE AND COLD WATER SWIM.

1. I love the sea and beach.

2. I love to swim and the feel of the water around me.

3. To see our beautiful planet from a more natural view point.

4. To enjoy the variety of the wildlife and the sea with all her faces.

5. The challenge. I love to push myself seeking to go ever further in less time.

6. The air. There is nothing so clean as pure sea air. I always work on my breathing. Aiming to breath as deeply in and as deeply out as I can. Breath in, pause and then breath in again .Im amazed how far the lungs will expand.

7. The Friendship. Water users of any description are a friendly bunch and always happy to natter and help.

8. The shear exuberance of swimming under the sun. It's just bliss.

9. Far from the Maddening crowd. After a 3 or 4hr swim I really feel like I've had a break from regular life.

10. The water totally supports you. So I don't have to worry about tripping, banging myself or falling over.

11. The after swim glow of tingling body and exercised limbs.

12. The happiness factor. There's definitely a link to cold water swimming and lifting of one's mood. If you are happy when you get in you're happier again when you leave the water. Or if you are below mood for whatever reason a good swim will help lift you and often restores the happy vibe completely.

I think every swimmer if they are honest will admit there are times when you just don't fancy it. I have found that 99% of the time if you just ignore that feeling and get in you will enjoy it.

As for the other 1% well give yourself a break because.....yes you've got it.....

There's always another day and another swim.

13. The unusual and the spectacular. The distance swim can produce the most amazing and thrilling gifts of nature.

I remember one day I was coming to the end of a 4 hr swim and suddenly a heavy hail shower rained down on the water. It was like a cacophony of a 1000 clapping hands congratulating me on a swim well swum. The hail stones danced and pivoted around in the most delightful pattern. I visualised that I had crossed the finish line and was welcomed by thunderous clapping. It made my heart sing and I laughed out loud.

Another time I turned to change direction and there was the most perfect double rainbow only visible to me for 5,4,3,2,1 secs and it was gone. Truly a gift from nature.

14. A sense of achievement and focus.

15. A constant learning experience. I am learning and experiencing new things which keeps it interesting. The biggest constant lesson is about the tides, currents and waves. I would love to become an expert in these because they can

make or break a swim and a reliable knowledge of them is the essence of safety.

16. The salt water has had the most wonderful affect on my skin making it brighter and moist. The constant movement of the waves and sea gently and sometimes not so gently exfoliating your skin makes it silky smooth.

17. It affords me to build a lifetime of memories of amazing sea time experiences. So if I'm confined or away for any reason I can reflect and relive them. MAGIC.

18. The weeds and lichen which cover the abrasion platforms. I love the colours and

textures of all the different weeds and their angelic dancing in the sea.

19. The variety. No 2 swims are the same and the antiscipation of yet another new adventure is addictive.

20. The Edginess. No distance swim is 100% guaranteed to be safe BUT that's the appeal and is very enlivening and stimulating.

21. The UNKNOWN

22. Distance swimming is a wonderful stress buster. The sea is the perfect place to go rant, rave or cry. To step back from the human and swim into the natural is very therapeutic.

23. The feel, sparkle and cleanliness of that Sun and Sea combination.

24. knowing that I am actively doing something to maintain my health and mental well being.

25. Helps me to maintain a healthy weight and conditions my muscles. I will never be as slim as I was before my babies but my size 18 is very useful to my swim. I seldom get frozen.

26. For the hell of it. Just for the hell of it!!.

27. It's free and limitless. You can swim as often as you like, where you like and for as long as you like. Bargain!

28. It appeals to my free spirit and I can do it my way. A swim should be personal and tailor made.

29. I love the feel of deep water around and beneath me.

30. It balances my sense of this World. Man's environment and rules are just one dimension of this Earth. Much is happening around us that we are not even aware of.

Mylor marina.

CHAPTER 9. MAKING A DISTANCE SWIM

It's definitely the distance that I love in cold water swimming. There's always a part of me that wants to go further. It's the challenge I enjoy and seeing the Natural world far from the Maddening crowd.

Apart from 2yrs in Australia and 3 in Africa. I have always lived in Cornwall. I know the Falmouth beaches intimately so it's natural to swim here. I also swim in Mylor Creek and from Flushing beach.

So very early on I decided it would be a wonderful challenge to swim from home in Mylor to Swanpool beach a distance of approx 8 miles.

Of course I couldn't do this when I first started but the route was ideal because it naturally splits into

4 Sections.

1. Mylor Creek to Mylor harbour.

2. Mylor harbour to Flushing beach.

3. Flushing beach to Castle Point.

4. Castle Point to Swanpool beach.

Each section is a similar distance but has it's own challenges.

1. Mylor Creek is totally ruled by the tide. So it's a must that you start the swim at high tide. This gives you maximum water and you are not swimming against the incoming tide. This would be like swimming in a tidal pool with the sea coming in at a rate of knots. All very hard work.

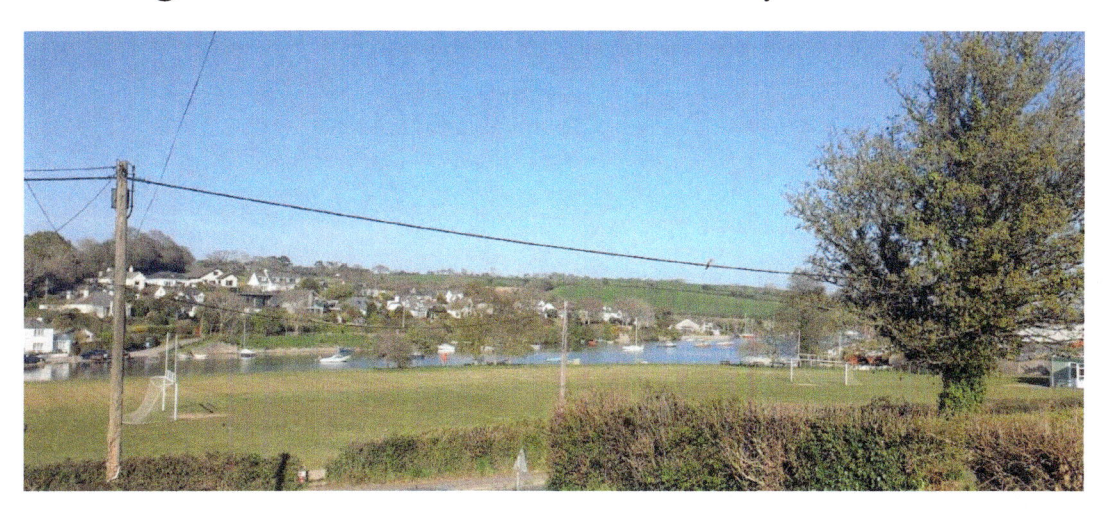

2. Once it's high tide there's an hours grace when the water doesn't move, allowing me to swim in relatively still water. When I reach Mylor harbour the water will be on the turn. The out going tide will now become an advantage as it will aid my swim. It travels at a rate of knots taking me with it. Mylor harbour to Flushing is in open sea and so the weather needs to be good with little or no wind.

Flushing beach is surprisingly clean considering there a full working docks opposite it.

3. Flushing to Castle point is dangerous because I am skirting the very edge of the shipping lanes. The swim itself is fine but it is the massive ships which come from Falmouth pier, Falmouth docks and The Super yacht boatyard which pose the problem. The tide by this time will be racing

out at a rate of knots which is vital if I am to get around Castle point.

The Harbour Master is king in this area and is responsible for the safety of all who use it. Although they don't totally ban swimming here they entreat you to swim else where. They state they can't guarantee the swimmers safety.

While on Flushing beach it's always interesting to see which boats are in dock .The Falmouth Packet newspaper tells the story of each of them.

The fact that I will swim just off shore is not taken into account.I do understand.

Little Dennis was built by Henry the Eighth in 1540-45.To guard the Carrick Roads. It was built on the remains of an Iron Age cliff Castle dating around 800bc.

4.FALMOUTH BAY The last final section of my chosen route is Falmouth Bay. The most wonderful basin of water ever. It stretches from Castle point to Swanpool beach and includes the award winning Gyllingvase and Castle Beaches. The water is crystal clear and just a fun place to swim. There's a resident solitary seal in the Bay as well as Nibbles who tends to hang out at Swanpool beach. The seals regularly join the swimmers and it's always a delight when they appear. These 2 are no way near as scary as Sammy who lives in Mylor creek. Sammy is an enormous male seal and is harmless but big...he's just BIG!! I still have not managed to get a photo of Sammy, to date he has evaded my camera I continue to try.....

So I designed this 4 stage route to develop my distance swimming. At first I would swim one section at a time. It's down to the weather and tide as to which route I tackle and when.

As I mentioned the river is hopeless if the tide is going out, it does actually go out completely at the top of the creek leaving thick slimy, smelly mud.

I remember when visitors didn't study the tide and they got their boat stuck in the mud. This time the coastguard and fire brigade made it a training exercise and launched a full scale rescue mission with numerous vehicles and umpteen personnel in attendance.

I've also known people who have chosen to sit it out and wait for the incoming tide rather than have the red faced embarrassment of admitting their error to the emergency services. Luckily they had supplies with them.

Each section has something different to offer. The creek is just so convenient I literally walk out of my gate, across the playing field and I'm there. At high tide the basin fills to overflowing and makes very pleasant swimming. There is some snobbery about swimming in the river. People will not swim there because they esteem it as dirty. There are 2 boatyards operating on the shores of the creek but I don't believe they discharge any oil or fuel into the river. There was also the mine disaster when a derelict mine flooded after 'end of the world rain' disgorging it's filthy metallic sludge into the waters of the area including Mylor Creek. But that was 20 plus years ago now. I work on the basis that if it's good enough for Sammy the seal (he has been a river resident for many years and looks the epitomy of good health) then its good enough for me.

Also this huge volume of water goes in and out, totally so we are left with bare mud in the upper creek not once but twice a day at a rapid rate of knots.

However I do concede that the river can smell a bit at times and there's lots of floating weed. As a precaution I never do front crawl or put my head under the water. After any swim I wash all my kit and have a thorough shower so all is well. To date I've never caught or suffered anything from the river and I don't even feel the need to cross my fingers as I write this. I see plenty of birds on the river. I think the most majestic are the herons. They are beauty and grace personified with their outrageously long legs and stream line bodies. We have a pair of resident swans that grace the river and delight everyone with their annual brood of signets. The whole village make it their business to care for the family and many people including myself feed them regularly.

We also have egrets, blackcaps, waxwings, redshanks and many more. And if you are very lucky you might just see a kingfisher.Surprisingly I saw 3 kingfisher when swimming at Swanpool this summer.It made me do a second take as the open sea is definitely not where you would usually find them, they prefer the sheltered tree lined shore of a river or creek. I can only conclude that they were passing through.

On the river you might meet a kayak or the occasional boat but they are easy to alert to your presence given the smaller area and they tend to stick to the middle of the river where the fastest current is.

No2.MYLOR YACHT HARBOUR TO FLUSHING.

This is a beautiful swim in the open sea. Ideally you want the tide to be going out on this stretch as it will carry you with it. Synchinising your stroke with the wave behind you can give you untold advantage in progress.

The route runs parallel to a popular walk across the fields to Flushing which is useful because you can chart your progress by counting off each field as you pass it.

This is where I'm most likely to have bouncy waves and where I will get seasick but not always.

There a bit of a rip current as you round the small headland to reach Flushing beach but nothing serious.

Flushing beach is a most beautiful beach which is divided into two by a large quay. It's where the locals go. It's unlikely that visitors to Cornwall will know it. The beach is a delight to small children as it has an abundance of shells and a safe shallow shoreline.

Flushing beach with Falmouth in the background

No3. FLUSHING TO CASTLE POINT. I will always be grateful for the experience of swimming from Flushing to Castle Point. It's a very edgy swim but thrilling. I tackled it at the crack of dawn and only met 2 fishing boats who easily saw me. The fishermen are usually very chirpy and rib me for being in the water and not in a boat.

A third boat freaked me out a little as it came straight at me. I moved and it followed. In the end with a prayer in my heart I stopped and waited. They came within 6 feet to me. Firstly they announced that they had been sent from the dock's security to check I was OK. Having established that I was fine they proceeded to lecture me about swimming so close to the big shipping lanes. I pointed out I was just passing through, only going one way and would be so tucked into the shore I definitely would not be a problem to any ship movement (tankers and kind cannot operate in 6 feet of water!) The security still argued that although they would allow me to continue it is hugely inappropriate to swim here.

On hindsight and after several conversations with the Harbour Master I agree with them and will remember this swim as a privileged and one off experience. It's important to listen to the experts and help where you can. I would hate to think my swim inspired others to adopt this route. Having said that the court is still out as to the new section I will adopt. The Falmouth Harbour is the 3rd most natural Harbour in the world. The deep water channel runs deep, deep, deep and is marked by huge buoys. To swim even on the very edge of the harbour was thrilling to me. I slipped effortlessly past Black rock. This is a iconic marker in Cornwall and very much an intrigue of my childhood. The name comes from a myth. The son of an Irish king was interrupted by the continuous barking of a seal as he was preaching. He was so frustrated at been drowned out by this raucous noise he threw a large black rock at the barking seal. It missed and the legend is, the rock remains wedged on top of a cluster of black rocks halfway across the harbour entrance. Today it is a popular site to spot seals basking in the sun. Black rock even features on the Falmouth Coat of Arms.

It was thrilling for me to swim past Black Rock even at a distance .I was surprised how big the collection of rocks are, they would certainly pose a threat to any Ship but are very well documented on all sea charts.

As I passed Black Rock I safely tucked into the shore only to be confronted by the horrid long weed .The weed is anchored to the seabed and stretches to just below or just on the surface of the sea. It's like long black tendrils which will delight to wrap around anything that comes within it's touch. I confess I withdrew a further 5 feet from the shore just to get away from its clutches. Above is a photo of the famous black rock.

By now the tide is flying out which is a real help in my progress. The sea was like a milpool not a wave insight . I love it like this. I was really hoping dolphins might swim along but sadly not today. On the shoreline is the Castle Point lookout, a very popular place for tourists and locals alike. I became aware of numerous people watching and discussing my progress. When I have an audience I subconsciously step up my effort. I know I do. They probably were impressed at the pace I was making but would likely not be aware of the oh so helpful tide which was racing out taking me with it.

In my heart I have locked away special treasury days and my one and only swim from Flushing beach to Castle point is definitely there along with my other precious joys.

CASTLE POINT. This is the headland that I must swim around to get to the Bay. It is a large turbulent area of water with cross and rip currents and angry tides. I have never known Castle Point to be still.

The Point has the magnificent fortress castle built from 1539 to 1545 by Henry the Eighth when England faced a possible invasion from Catholic Europe. There is a sister castle at St.Mawes opposite and together over the centuries they have guarded the open mouth of the Carrick Roads from hostile invasion such as the Great Amanda which thankfully never did come in the end.

These defences were again used in the first and second World war.

Local legend has it that in Henry's time there was a chain mail fencing stretching across from Castle to Castle to snare hostile craft. But I've never been able to source more information about it.

Section4. I love Falmouth Bay. Its huge with crystal clean seawater and no real obstacles like rocky outcrops or horrid floating weeds. The water is deep with primarily a sandy bottom. The Bay has many faces and I've marvelled how it presents itself in various weather conditions. I've seen it crystal blue with not a

Pendennis Castle .The low building in front is the Coastguard station.

ripple in sight but also on other days as a

raging angry body of grey/ black water as reflected from the sky above with massive waves which can toss any boat around. And all the in-betweens. It has some rip currents but they are not a huge problem and has the esteemed blue flag beach Gyllingvase.

The Bay is perfect for distance swimming and is an absolute swimmer's dream.

Falmouth Bay .

So this is my 4 sectioned route.

I have trained in building strength and experience. For the first training I swam a section at a time. Each section is approximately 2 miles long and has been a brilliant training ground. Of course no 2 swims are the same but over time I have come to know the area .

CHAPTER 10 THE IMPORTANCE OF A GOAL.

Like all things in life it's important to have a goal when distance swimming. You will almost certainly find you can't go from zero or fun swimming to any distance in one shot. So set goals personal to yourself. If you are swimming with a club they will have a planned staggered route to help you build the distance in stages. My staged swimming route is invaluable to me. There is something enchanting and inviting as I look to the distance. Knowing that very soon I will reach the area under my own power and strength. All swimmers will experience the thrill of anticipation for the forthcoming swim and adventure.

GETTING READY FOR THE SWIM.

Before I enter the water I will dress carefully to ensure I've not forgotten anything. In these winter months my dressing goes something like this:

1. Check your body i.e. are you hydrated, and have enough backed calories from the night

before? Have you peed and pooed one last time? While it's well known that a sneaky pee is unspoken of but acceptable you really don't want an accident with the latter. So save yourself the blush and go before you leave.

2.Next get the Vaseline out and anoint generously under the arms and all around the armpit. The groin area is recommended for men but I say ere on the side of caution girls and do it anyway. If you are wearing a wet suit put vaseline around the neck and anywhere else you might rub.

3. I wear a vest and shorts but no bra. Although a bra will make me look a better shape it causes horrendous chaffing. Go for safety rather than glamour. Trust me you will be glad you did.

4. Next on goes my thermals top and bottom.

5. Then my outer long sleeve top and leggings. All of this is pretty much skin tight but comfortable.

6. On my feet I have my sea boots. I found these cold to wear on their own so I wear thermal socks inside the boots. This ensures lovely toasty warm feet.

7. Oh how I wish the same could be said about my hands which can turn to ice blocks if not carefully tended. I'm experimenting with all sorts of liners and coverings but my hands are still only 80% warm. That's wearing sea mitts lined with thermal mitts. But I do now have my warming exercise when I play windmills in the sea to bring cold hands to acceptably warm again. Alternatively I've found butterfly stroke to be equally effective to warm your hands. So you maintain your swim too.

Do I need to tell you to keep one hand uncovered until you go into the sea?. Or are you smarter than me who even now will get fully togged up only to find I can't lock the car or reach in my pocket or put the bike chain on.

What to do with the car keys is a problem but you can buy a container which locks onto the car wheel.

I will never put valuables in my buoy. Never have, never will.

8. Any sunscreen should be applied and a hat or cap of your choice. Swimmers often wear 2 caps in Winter.

9. Some swimmers wear ear plugs which are cheap to buy and can help stop you developing glue ear. And some wear nose clips.

10. The most important pieces of equipment are my buoy and whistle. I take the time to check my buoy i.e., inflated ,named, next of kin written on it and no leaks.

Some hardy swimmers would laugh at this long list as they just wear swimming suits and trunks. Wow I salute them and note their truly reddened skin as they exit the water. I don't know any distance swimmers that only wear swim suits in the Winter.

Just an after thought. After spreading the vaseline I will massage my face and hands with the residue. An eminent lady consultant dermatologist was asked what she recommended ladies should use on their face. The doctor shocked the Seminar by stating firmly that common Vaseline does wonders for the face skin. I agree having taken her advice but I would work it well in your hands before you apply it or it will be very sticky on your face.

When applying the vaseline to your face do be careful not to get it near your eyes. It can cause salt to stick to the grease and can result in sore and swollen eyes.

USING MY TRAINING ROUTE.

So I have my 4 section route which I use to train and enjoy the distance swim. For all of the summer I would do a section at a time. Each section is approximately 2 miles long and gives me the opportunity to build my stamina and strength. For example swimming in the comparatively calm river is a total contrast to swimming in the open sea from Mylor Harbour to Flushing and this allows me to develop different skills in a variety of conditions.

Having settled on a route I choose a goal of both time and purpose.

I decided that I would swim the full 4 section swim on Easter Bank Holiday Monday in aid of Motor Neuron Disease research. It would be part of a big fund raising event. Why MND? Well I was tested for MND and other nasties about 8 years ago. I fall over for no reason and choke while eating and have other tiresome symptoms. On examination the Neurologist established I have a problem. He said they would do a barrage of tests but it was likely I would have to be retested at a later date. Nothing prepares you for such possibility especially coming from a medical background and family I understood these type of diseases and all their ugliness fairly well. I wasn't so much scared of dying because I'm certain life goes on beyond the grave but the thought of being reduced to sans teeth, sans mind ,sans everything terrified me.

However I received help from a surprising source. It was about the time that Stephen Hawking's film was released. I went on my own to see it and was totally blown away by the sheer fortitude of this remarkable man. Against all odds Stephen lived to be 76 and with help lived a life of excellence and achievement. He always maintained that it was vital to concentrate on what you Can do, not on what you've lost.

I am by nature a positive person and people have described me as a force to be reckoned with.

I left the Cinema with just one thought.......

IF STEPHEN CAN DO IT I CAN !

I have dedicated this book to Stephen Hawking and his family as a thank you for his outstanding shining example which helped rescue me. As I mentioned I never did more tests but I settled to fund raise for MND because it's a merciless disease and causes optimum misery.

From then on I set about blanking my symptoms and problems. Not giving them any energy or focus in my life. Inspired by my daughter Sarah I did a massive juicing reboot for weeks using the very best ingredients. When I met Joe Cross in London I was bubbling over with enthusiasm about how much juicing has helped me. Of course it hasn't changed the symptoms but the nourishment and vitality it gives my body is astonishing and contributes to keeping things under wraps.

My first set of tests came back with symptoms but more tests would be needed. I've only once been back to the hospital after a serious choking incident but I thought how pointless it all was given that nothing can be done anyway and have not been back since. I prefer to concentrate on life and beauty and acting on the assumption of being well. Not giving energy to this destructive force within me. If I fall over I get up with the absolute minimum of fuss. I don't talk about it, I don't accept help. I just focus on literally freezing it out of my life. I laugh when my weaker right side causes me after a long swim to start circling rather than going forward. Concentrated arm strokes is the answer.

There is a scripture in the Bible which states the Spirit can heal the physical and this certainly seems to be working for me.

The thought system The Secret really works in every aspect of life and has helped me to seize the day xx

You can find it on You tube.

Having said all this I am aware not everyone is so fortunate and I really want to give something back and raise as much money as possible for Research. I have a beautifully painted portrait of Stephen by the talented artist Gillon Lockett and feel a joyful thanks and total respect everytime I look at it.

STEPHEN HAWKING I SALUTE YOU xx

And what of tomorrow? Will my symptoms finally catch up with me one day? One verse of scripture answers this..

Take no thought for tomorrow for the morrow shall take thought for itself.

Sufficient unto the day is the evil there of.

Matt:6:34. Having a meltdown? Have a prayer .

I went in search of snow in New York and Salt Lake City with little success. But 2 weeks after getting home the Cornish

weather delivered and this time it was deep.

The harbour with a snowy Falmouth.

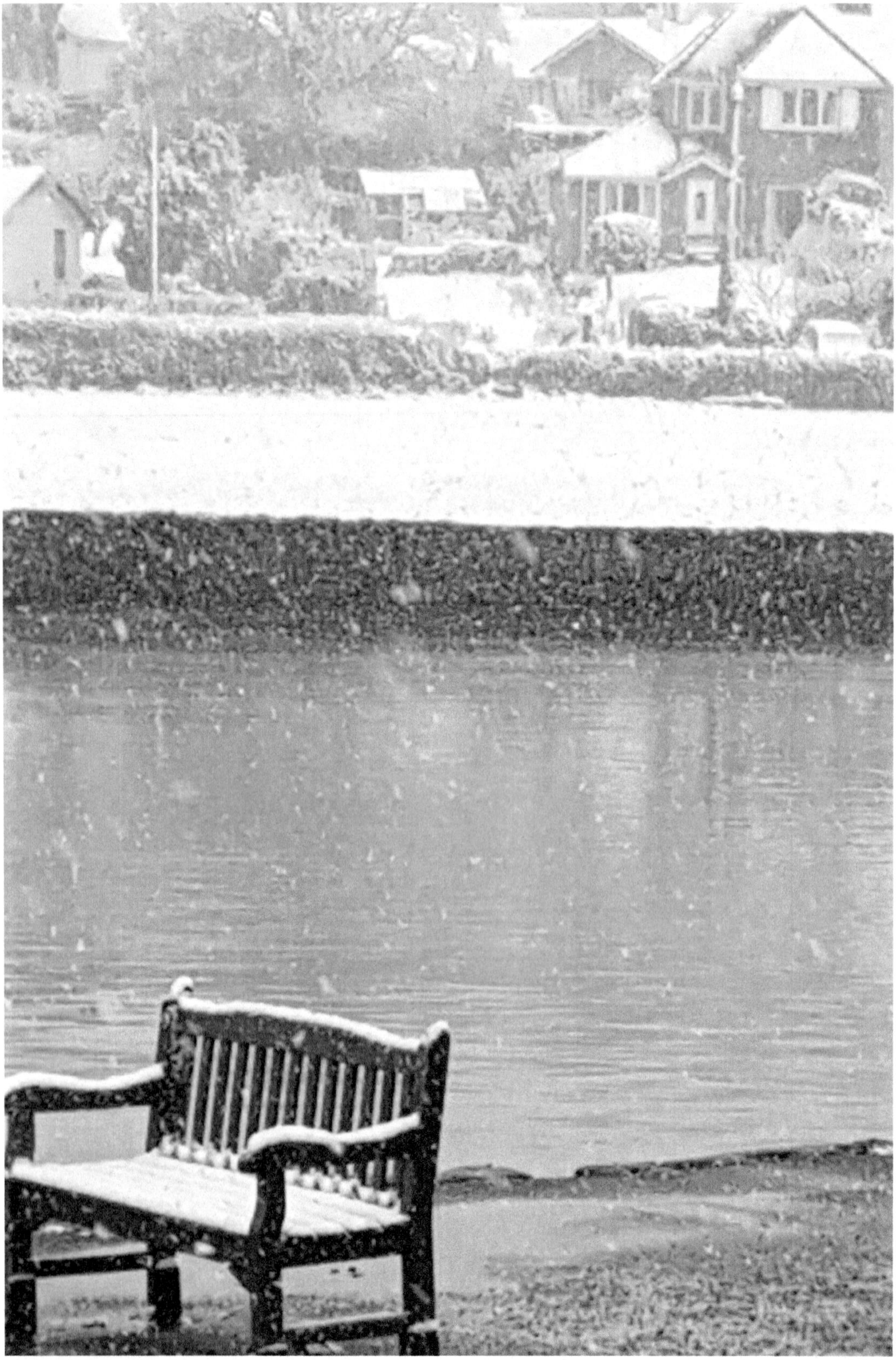

The experts at David Austen said that the extreme cold in the winter had caused my rose to produce a bud within it's flower. How strange.

HOORAY FOR THE CORNISH WEATHER

This heavy snow is very rare for Cornwall. When my children were young we would go in search of snow. This was usually past Bodmin in Cornwall which is higher.

But it's so exciting and fun when we have snow like this.

I have lived in the village for 33 years and can only remember less than a handful of proper snow episodes. I do remember the edges of the creek freezing and the shore line covered in frosty snow.

A SALTY HAT AND I.EPILOGUE.

THE FUTURE.... So now it's mid- February and my fellow swimmers and I have survived January swimming. Hew, at times it has been bitterly cold.

The last distance swim of Flushing to Swanpool was supposed to be followed up with intense swimming and training in the pool but then lockdown happened and all health centres and hotels closed. Throughout Winter the most I have been able to swim is 2 miles at a time as it's just too cold. Conditions can change and in the Winter they are more likely to change for the worse. This coupled with a serious risk of hypothermia means that distance swimming is not an option. But hey I still get a good work out in the water and can be more social with my fellow swimmers.

I have had to prospone my swim and fund raising event for MND research until 2022 as I think Covid is likely to dominate the rest of this year 2021. And so I along with all distance swimmers wait for the warmer climes of Spring and Summer to resume our distance.

So there we have it. I hope you've enjoyed A Salty Hat and I as much as I have enjoyed writing it. All this information and pearls of wisdom and advice are by and large things I wish I knew when I started distance swimming. I hope as well that I have given you a flavour of the shear joy of wild swimming and the beauty of Cornwall. I think it's so important to discover what works for you. Be guided by others and the professionals but ultimately you are the author of Your distance swim. You might think to do things a little differently from the throng but hey so long as you're safe it's OK. Be your own person.

NEVER ASK PERMISSION TO BE YOURSELF.

Jam or Cream first? The age old argument. Which

JAM FIRST!

comes first the jam or the cream? In Cornwall it absolutely has to be jam first .No discussion, no doubt. Tradition says jam first! It also says that to be absolutely correct It should be served on splits. Its not totally clear when the cream tea started but there are records to suggest it could be as early as the 11th century.

Carmen Vigo is a life time and distance swimmer.With a joy of life and steely determination Carmen has made the most of her health and has her mind set firmly on swimming the Channel and braving the cold to swim in Antarctica. But not before she raises 100,000 pounds, for Research into MND.(research is expensive)

TODAY WE WILL DO THE EXTRAORDINARY. Xx

Printed in Great Britain
by Amazon